Navigation Rules and Regulations Handbook

Containing   - International and Inland Rules of the Road
and their respective Annexes
- Bridge-to-Bridge Radiotelephone Regulations
- Vessel Traffic Management Regulations
- Other pertinent regulations for waterway users

Prepared by
Department of Homeland Security
& United States Coast Guard

Presented by
Paradise Cay Publications Inc.
PO Box 29
Arcata, CA 95518-0029

Phone   (707) 822-9063
Fax   (707) 822-9163
orders@paracay.com
www.paracay.com

RECORD OF CHANGES

CHANGE NUMBER	DATE OF CHANGE	DATE EFFECTIVE	BY WHOM ENTERED
001	17NOV2014 / 22NOV2014	17NOV2014 / 22NOV2014	LNM 46-14 / NTM 48-14
002	8DEC2014 / 20DEC2014	8DEC2014 / 20DEC2014	LNM 49-14 / NTM 51-14
003	24AUG2015/ 14SEPT2015	24AUG2015 / 14SEPT2015	LNM 35-15 / NTM 37-15
004	21SEPT2015/ 5OCT2015	21SEPT2015/ 5OCT2015	LNM 39-15 / NTM 41-15
005	30NOV2015/ 12DEC2015	30NOV2015/ 12DEC2015	LNM 48-15 / NTM 50-15

Corrections published and recorded here are annotated by a double underline and line in the left margin (like this) and are italicized.

CONTENTS‡

---

‡ Footnotes proceeded by the double-dagger (‡) symbol indicates clarifications added by the U.S. Coast Guard Office of Navigation Systems; and, are not found in the original source material.

INTRODUCTION

International Rules

The International Rules in this book were formalized in the Convention on the International Regulations for Preventing Collisions at Sea, 1972, and became effective on July 15, 1977. The Rules (commonly called 72 COLREGS) are part of the Convention, and vessels flying the flags of states ratifying the treaty are bound to the Rules. The United States has ratified this treaty and all United States flag vessels must adhere to these Rules where applicable. President Gerald R. Ford proclaimed 72 COLREGS and the Congress adopted them as the International Navigational Rules Act of 1977.

The 72 COLREGS were developed by the Inter-Governmental Maritime Consultative Organization (IMCO) which in May 1982 was renamed the International Maritime Organization (IMO). In November 1981, IMO's Assembly adopted 55 amendments to the 72 COLREGS which became effective on June 16, 1983. The IMO also adopted 9 more amendments which became effective on June 29, 1989. A single amendment became effective March 19, 1991. In 1993 8 amendments were adopted by the IMO which entered into force in 1995. The IMO adopted 9 amendments which entered into force November 29, 2003. Lastly, a single amendment was adopted which updated the Distress signals and entered into force on December 1, 2009. The International Rules in this book contain these amendments.

These Rules are applicable on waters outside of established navigational lines of demarcation. The lines are called COLREGS Demarcation Lines and delineate those waters upon which mariners shall comply with the Inland and International Rules. COLREGS Demarcation Lines are contained in this book.

INTRODUCTION

Inland Regulations

The Inland Rules in this book replace the old Inland Rules, Western Rivers Rules, Great Lakes Rules, their respective pilot rules and interpretive rules, and parts of the Motorboat Act of 1940. Many of the old navigation rules were originally enacted in the 1800's. Occasionally, provisions were added to cope with the increasing complexities of water transportation. Eventually, the navigation rules for United States inland waterways became such a confusing patchwork of requirements that in the 1960's several attempts were made to revise and simplify them. These attempts were not successful.

Following the signing of the Convention on the International Regulations for Preventing Collisions at Sea, 1972, a new effort was made to unify and update the various inland navigation rules. This effort culminated in the enactment of the Inland Navigational Rules Act of 1980. This legislation sets out Rules 1 through 38 - the main body of the Rules. The five Annexes were published as regulations. It is important to note that with the exception of Annex V to the Inland Rules, the International and Inland Rules and Annexes are very similar in both content and format.

The effective date for the Inland Navigation Rules was December 24, 1981, except for the Great Lakes where the effective date was March 1, 1983.

On May 17, 2010 the US Coast Guard published a Final Rule which placed the Inland Navigational Rules into the Code of Federal Regulations. This move was in accordance with the Coast Guard and Maritime Transportation Act of 2004, which repealed the Inland Navigation Rules as they appeared in United States Code.

This Handbook supersedes Commandant Instruction M16672.2D, *Navigation Rules: International–Inland.* It maintains the same format and provides additional and updated content. Not all U.S. Navigation Regulations found in Title 33 of the Code of Federal Regulations are contained in this handbook.

LEGAL CITATIONS

72 COLREGS
International Navigational Rules .... Public Law 95-75;
 Act of 1977 .... 91 Stat 308;
.... 33 U.S.C. 1601-1608

COLREGS Demarcation Lines .... 33 CFR 80
72 COLREGS: Implementing Rules .... 33 CFR 81
72 COLREGS: Interpretative Rules .... 33 CFR 82
Amendments to 72 COLREGS Effective June 1, 1983 . 48 FR 28634
COLREGS Penalty Provisions ....33 U.S.C. 1608

INLAND RULES
Inland Navigational Rules Act of 1980 .... Public Law 96-591;
.... 94 Stat 3415;
.... 33 CFR 83

Annex I: Positioning and Technical
 Details of Lights and Shapes .... 33 CFR 84
Annex II: Additional Signals for Fishing in Close Proximity 33 CFR 85
Annex III: Technical Details of Sound Signal Appliances . 33 CFR 86
Annex IV: Distress Signals .... 33 CFR 87
Annex V: Pilot Rules .... 33 CFR 88

Inland Navigation Rules: Implementing Rules .... 33 CFR 89
Inland Navigation Rules: Interpretative Rules .... 33 CFR 90
Boundary Lines .... 46 CFR 7

Inland Rules Penalty Provisions ....33 U.S.C. 2072

VESSEL NAVIGATON REGULATIONS
Vessel Bridge-to-Bridge Radiotelephone Act .... Public Law 92-63;
.... 85 Stat.164;
.... 33 U.S.C. 1201-1208
Vessel Bridge-to-Bridge Radiotelephone Regulations ..... 33 CFR 26
Other FCC Regulations Pertaining to
 Maritime Communications .... 47 CFR 80.1001-80.1023
Vessel Traffic Management .... 33 CFR 161

OPERATIONS OF VESSELS GENERALLY
Penalties for Negligent Operations .... 33 U.S.C. 2302
Duties Related to Marine Casualty .... 33 U.S.C. 2303
Duty to Provide Assistance at Sea .... 33 U.S.C. 2304
Vessel Reporting Requirements .... 33 U.S.C. 2306

CONVERSION TABLE

Conversion of Metric to U.S. Customary/Imperial Units

Metric Measure	U.S. Customary/ Imperial Measure (approximately)
1,000 Meters (M)	3,280.8 ft.
500 M	1,640.4 ft.
200 M	656.2 ft.
150 M	492.1 ft.
100 M	328.1 ft.
75 M	246.1 ft.
60 M	196.8 ft.
50 M	164.0 ft.
25 M	82.0 ft.
20 M	65.6 ft.
12 M	39.4 ft.
10 M	32.8 ft.
8 M	26.2 ft.
7 M	23.0 ft.
6 M	19.7 ft.
5 M	16.4 ft.
4.5 M	14.8 ft.
4.0 M	13.1 ft.
3.5 M	11.5 ft.
2.5 M	8.2 ft.
2.0 M	6.6 ft.
1.5 M	4.9 ft.
1.0 M	3.3 ft.
0.9 M	35.4 in.
0.6 M	23.6 in.
0.5 M	19.7 in.
300 Millimeters (mm)	11.8 in.
200 mm	7.9 in.

NAVIGATION RULES

INTERNATIONAL—INLAND

—INTERNATIONAL—
General

PART A—GENERAL

Rule 1
Application

(a) These Rules shall apply to all vessels upon the high seas and in all waters connected therewith navigable by seagoing vessels.

(b) Nothing in these Rules shall interfere with the operation of special rules made by an appropriate authority for roadsteads, harbors, rivers, lakes or inland waterways connected with the high seas and navigable by seagoing vessels. Such special rules shall conform as closely as possible to these Rules.

(c) Nothing in these Rules shall interfere with the operation of any special rules made by the Government of any State with respect to additional station or signal lights, shapes or whistle signals for ships of war and vessels proceeding under convoy, or with respect to additional station or signal lights or shapes for fishing vessels engaged in fishing as a fleet. These additional station or signal lights, shapes or whistle signals shall, so far as possible, be such that they cannot be mistaken for any light, shape or signal authorized elsewhere under these Rules[‡].

(d) Traffic separation schemes may be adopted by the Organization for the purpose of these Rules.

[‡] Submarines may display, as a distinctive means of identification, an intermittent flashing amber (yellow) beacon with a sequence of one flash per second for three (3) seconds followed by a three (3) second off-period (32 CFR 707.7). Other special rules made by the Secretary of the Navy with respect to additional station and signal lights are found in Part 706 of Title 32, Code of Federal Regulations (32 CFR 706).

—INLAND—
General
33 CFR 83
SUBPART A—GENERAL

Rule 1
Application

§ 83.01

(a) These Rules apply to all vessels upon the inland waters of the United States, and to vessels of the United States on the Canadian waters of the Great Lakes to the extent that there is no conflict with Canadian law. The regulations in this subchapter (subchapter E, 33 CFR parts 83 through 90) have preemptive effect over State or local regulation within the same field.

(b) (i)These Rules constitute special rules made by an appropriate authority within the meaning of Rule 1(b) of the International Regulations for Preventing Collisions at Sea, 1972, including annexes currently in force for the United States ("International Regulations").

(ii) All vessels complying with the construction and equipment requirements of the International Regulations are considered to be in compliance with these Rules.

(c) Nothing in these Rules shall interfere with the operation of any special rules made by the Secretary of the Navy with respect to additional station or signal lights and shapes or whistle signals for ships of war and vessels proceeding under convoy, or by the Secretary with respect to additional station or signal lights and shapes for fishing vessels engaged in fishing as a fleet. These additional station or signal lights and shapes or whistle signals shall, so far as possible, be such that they cannot be mistaken for any light, shape, or signal authorized elsewhere under these Rules. Notice of such special rules shall be published in the Federal Register and, after the effective date specified in such notice, they shall have effect as if they were a part of these Rules[‡].

(d) Traffic separation schemes may be established for the purposes of these Rules. Vessel traffic service regulations may be in effect in certain areas.

[‡] Submarines may display, as a distinctive means of identification, an intermittent flashing amber (yellow) beacon with a sequence of one flash per second for three (3) seconds followed by a three (3) second off-period (32 CFR 707.7). Other special rules made by the Secretary of the Navy with respect to additional station and signal lights are found in Part 706 of Title 32, Code of Federal Regulations (32 CFR 706).

Rule 1—CONTINUED

(e) Whenever the Government concerned shall have determined that a vessel of special construction or purpose cannot comply fully with the provisions of any of these Rules with respect to the number, position, range or arc of visibility of lights or shapes, as well as to the disposition and characteristics of sound-signaling appliances, such vessel shall comply with such other provisions in regard to the number, position, range or arc of visibility of lights or shapes, as well as to the disposition and characteristics of sound-signaling appliances, as her Government shall have determined to be the closest possible compliance with these Rules in respect to that vessel.

Rule 2
Responsibility

(a) Nothing in these Rules shall exonerate any vessel, or the owner, master or crew thereof, from the consequences of any neglect to comply with these Rules or of the neglect of any precaution which may be required by the ordinary practice of seamen, or by the special circumstances of the case.

(b) In construing and complying with these Rules due regard shall be had to all dangers of navigation and collision and to any special circumstances, including the limitations of the vessels involved, which may make a departure from these Rules necessary to avoid immediate danger.

—INLAND—
General

Rule 1—CONTINUED

(e) Whenever the Secretary determines that a vessel or class of vessels of special construction or purpose cannot comply fully with the provisions of any of these Rules with respect to the number, position, range, or arc of visibility of lights or shapes, as well as to the disposition and characteristics of sound-signaling appliances, the vessel shall comply with such other provisions in regard to the number, position, range, or arc of visibility of lights or shapes, as well as to the disposition and characteristics of sound-signaling appliances, as the Secretary shall have determined to be the closest possible compliance with these Rules. The Secretary may issue a certificate of alternative compliance for a vessel or class of vessels specifying the closest possible compliance with these Rules. The Secretary of the Navy shall make these determinations and issue certificates of alternative compliance for vessels of the Navy.

(f) The Secretary may accept a certificate of alternative compliance issued by a contracting party to the International Regulations if it determines that the alternative compliance standards of the contracting party are substantially the same as those of the United States.

(g) The operator of each self-propelled vessel 12 meters or more in length shall carry, on board and maintain for ready reference, a copy of these Rules.

Rule 2
Responsibility

§ 83.02

(a) Nothing in these Rules shall exonerate any vessel, or the owner, master, or crew thereof, from the consequences of any neglect to comply with these Rules or of the neglect of any precaution which may be required by the ordinary practice of seamen, or by the special circumstances of the case.

(b) In construing and complying with these Rules due regard shall be had to all dangers of navigation and collision and to any special circumstances, including the limitations of the vessels involved, which may make a departure from these Rules necessary to avoid immediate danger.

—INTERNATIONAL—
General

Rule 3
General Definitions

For the purpose of these Rules, except where the context otherwise requires:

(a) The word *vessel* includes every description of water craft, including non-displacement craft, WIG craft and seaplanes, used or capable of being used as a means of transportation on water.

(b) The term *power-driven vessel* means any vessel propelled by machinery.

(c) The term *sailing vessel* means any vessel under sail provided that propelling machinery, if fitted, is not being used.

(d) The term *vessel engaged in fishing* means any vessel fishing with nets, lines, trawls or other fishing apparatus which restrict maneuverability, but does not include a vessel fishing with trolling lines or other fishing apparatus which do not restrict maneuverability.

(e) The word *seaplane* includes any aircraft designed to maneuver on the water.

(f) The term *vessel not under command* means a vessel which through some exceptional circumstance is unable to maneuver as required by these Rules and is therefore unable to keep out of the way of another vessel.

(g) The term *vessel restricted in her ability to maneuver* means a vessel which from the nature of her work is restricted in her ability to maneuver as required by these Rules and is therefore unable to keep out of the way of another vessel. The term *vessels restricted in their ability to maneuver* shall include but not be limited to:

(i) a vessel engaged in laying, servicing or picking up a navigation mark, submarine cable or pipeline;

(ii) a vessel engaged in dredging, surveying or underwater operations;

(iii) a vessel engaged in replenishment or transferring persons, provisions or cargo while underway;

(iv) a vessel engaged in the launching or recovery of aircraft;

(v) a vessel engaged in mine clearance operations;

(vi) a vessel engaged in a towing operation such as severely restricts the towing vessel and her tow in their ability to deviate from their course.

(h) The term *vessel constrained by her draft* means a power-driven vessel which, because of her draft in relation to the available depth and width of navigable water is severely restricted in her ability to deviate from the course she is following.

—INLAND—
General

Rule 3
General definitions

§ 83.03

For the purpose of these Rules and Subchapter E‡, except where the context otherwise requires:

(a) The word *vessel* includes every description of water craft, including non-displacement craft, WIG craft and seaplanes, used or capable of being used as a means of transportation on water.

(b) The term *power-driven vessel* means any vessel propelled by machinery.

(c) The term *sailing vessel* means any vessel under sail provided that propelling machinery, if fitted, is not being used.

(d) The term *vessel engaged in fishing* means any vessel fishing with nets, lines, trawls, or other fishing apparatus which restricts maneuverability, but does not include a vessel fishing with trolling lines or other fishing apparatus which do not restrict maneuverability.

(e) The word *seaplane* includes any aircraft designed to maneuver on the water.

(f) The term *vessel not under command* means a vessel which through some exceptional circumstance is unable to maneuver as required by these Rules and is therefore unable to keep out of the way of another vessel.

(g) The term *vessel restricted in her ability to maneuver* means a vessel which, from the nature of her work, is restricted in her ability to maneuver as required by these Rules and is therefore unable to keep out of the way of another vessel. The term *vessels restricted in their ability to maneuver* include, but are not limited to:

(i) A vessel engaged in laying, servicing or picking up a navigation mark, submarine cable, or pipeline;

(ii) a vessel engaged in dredging, surveying, or underwater operations;

(iii) a vessel engaged in replenishment or transferring persons, provisions, or cargo while underway;

(iv) a vessel engaged in the launching or recovery of aircraft;

(v) a vessel engaged in mine clearance operations;

(vi) a vessel engaged in a towing operation such as severely restricts the towing vessel and her tow in their ability to deviate from their course.

(h) [Reserved]

---

‡ Parts 83-90 of Title 33 Code of Federal Regulations.

Rule 3—CONTINUED

(i) The word *underway* means that a vessel is not at anchor, or made fast to the shore, or aground.

(j) The words *length* and *breadth* of a vessel mean her length overall and greatest breadth.

(k) Vessels shall be deemed to be in sight of one another only when one can be observed visually from the other.

(l) The term *restricted visibility* means any condition in which visibility is restricted by fog, mist, falling snow, heavy rainstorms, sandstorms or any other similar causes.

(m) The term *Wing-In-Ground (WIG) craft* means a multimodal craft which, in its main operational mode, flies in close proximity to the surface by utilizing surface-effect action.

—INLAND—
General

Rule 3—CONTINUED

(i) The word *underway* means that a vessel is not at anchor, or made fast to the shore, or aground.

(j) The words *length* and *breadth* of a vessel mean her length overall and greatest breadth.

(k) Vessels shall be deemed to be in sight of one another only when one can be observed visually from the other.

(l) The term *restricted visibility* means any condition in which visibility is restricted by fog, mist, falling snow, heavy rainstorms, sandstorms, or any other similar causes.

(m) The term *Wing-In-Ground* (WIG) craft means a multimodal craft which, in its main operational mode, flies in close proximity to the surface by utilizing surface-effect action.

(n) *Western Rivers* means the Mississippi River, its tributaries, South Pass, and Southwest Pass, to the navigational demarcation lines dividing the high seas from harbors, rivers, and other inland waters of the United States, and the Port Allen-Morgan City Alternate Route, and that part of the Atchafalaya River above its junction with the Port Allen-Morgan City Alternate Route including the Old River and the Red River.

(o) *Great Lakes* means the Great Lakes and their connecting and tributary waters including the Calumet River as far as the Thomas J. O'Brien Lock and Controlling Works (between mile 326 and 327), the Chicago River as far as the east side of the Ashland Avenue Bridge (between mile 321 and 322), and the Saint Lawrence River as far east as the lower exit of Saint Lambert Lock.

(p) *Secretary* means the Secretary of the Department in which the Coast Guard is operating.

(q) *Inland Waters* means the navigable waters of the United States shoreward of the navigational demarcation lines dividing the high seas from harbors, rivers, and other inland waters of the United States and the waters of the Great Lakes on the United States side of the International Boundary.

(r) *Inland Rules* or *Rules* means these Inland Navigational Rules and the annexes thereto, which govern the conduct of vessels and specify the lights, shapes, and sound signals that apply on inland waters.

(s) *International Regulations* means the International Regulations for Preventing Collisions at Sea, 1972, including annexes currently in force for the United States.

—INTERNATIONAL—
Steering and Sailing Rules

PART B—STEERING AND SAILING RULES

Section I—Conduct of Vessels in Any Condition of Visibility

Rule 4
Application

Rules in this Section apply to any condition of visibility.

Rule 5
Look-out

Every vessel shall at all times maintain a proper look-out by sight and hearing as well as by all available means appropriate in the prevailing circumstances and conditions so as to make a full appraisal of the situation and of the risk of collision.

—INLAND—
Steering and Sailing Rules

SUBPART B—STEERING AND SAILING RULES

Conduct of Vessels in Any Condition of Visibility

Rule 4
Application
§ 83.04

Rules 4 through 10 (§§ 83.04 through 83.10) apply in any condition of visibility.

Rule 5
Look-out
§ 83.05

Every vessel shall at all times maintain a proper look-out by sight and hearing as well as by all available means appropriate in the prevailing circumstances and conditions so as to make a full appraisal of the situation and of the risk of collision.

—INTERNATIONAL—
Steering and Sailing Rules

Rule 6
Safe Speed

Every vessel shall at all times proceed at a safe speed so that she can take proper and effective action to avoid collision and be stopped within a distance appropriate to the prevailing circumstances and conditions.

In determining a safe speed the following factors shall be among those taken into account:

(a) By all vessels:

(i) the state of visibility;

(ii) the traffic density including concentrations of fishing vessels or any other vessels;

(iii) the maneuverability of the vessel with special reference to stopping distance and turning ability in the prevailing conditions;

(iv) at night, the presence of background light such as from shore lights or from back scatter of her own lights;

(v) the state of wind, sea and current, and the proximity of navigational hazards;

(vi) the draft in relation to the available depth of water.

(b) Additionally, by vessels with operational radar:

(i) the characteristics, efficiency and limitations of the radar equipment;

(ii) any constraints imposed by the radar range scale in use;

(iii) the effect on radar detection of the sea state, weather and other sources of interference;

(iv) the possibility that small vessels, ice and other floating objects may not be detected by radar at an adequate range;

(v) the number, location and movement of vessels detected by radar;

(vi) the more exact assessment of the visibility that may be possible when radar is used to determine the range of vessels or other objects in the vicinity.

—INLAND—
Steering and Sailing Rules

Rule 6
Safe speed

§ 83.06

Every vessel shall at all times proceed at a safe speed so that she can take proper and effective action to avoid collision and be stopped within a distance appropriate to the prevailing circumstances and conditions.

In determining a safe speed the following factors shall be among those taken into account:

(a) By all vessels:

(i) The state of visibility;

(ii) The traffic density including concentration of fishing vessels or any other vessels;

(iii) The maneuverability of the vessel with special reference to stopping distance and turning ability in the prevailing conditions;

(iv) At night, the presence of background light such as from shore lights or from back scatter of her own lights;

(v) The state of wind, sea, and current, and the proximity of navigational hazards;

(vi) The draft in relation to the available depth of water.

(b) Additionally, by vessels with operational radar:

(i) The characteristics, efficiency and limitations of the radar equipment;

(ii) Any constraints imposed by the radar range scale in use;

(iii) The effect on radar detection of the sea state, weather, and other sources of interference;

(iv) The possibility that small vessels, ice and other floating objects may not be detected by radar at an adequate range;

(v) The number, location, and movement of vessels detected by radar;

(vi) The more exact assessment of the visibility that may be possible when radar is used to determine the range of vessels or other objects in the vicinity.

—INTERNATIONAL—
Steering and Sailing Rules

Rule 7
Risk of Collision

(a) Every vessel shall use all available means appropriate to the prevailing circumstances and conditions to determine if risk of collision exists. If there is any doubt such risk shall be deemed to exist.

(b) Proper use shall be made of radar equipment if fitted and operational, including long-range scanning to obtain early warning of risk of collision and radar plotting or equivalent systematic observation of detected objects.

(c) Assumptions shall not be made on the basis of scanty information, especially scanty radar information.

(d) In determining if risk of collision exists the following considerations shall be among those taken into account:

(i) such risk shall be deemed to exist if the compass bearing of an approaching vessel does not appreciably change;

(ii) such risk may sometimes exist even when an appreciable bearing change is evident, particularly when approaching a very large vessel or a tow or when approaching a vessel at close range.

—INLAND—
Steering and Sailing Rules

Rule 7
Risk of collision

§ 83.07

(a) Every vessel shall use all available means appropriate to the prevailing circumstances and conditions to determine if risk of collision exists. If there is any doubt such risk shall be deemed to exist.

(b) Proper use shall be made of radar equipment if fitted and operational, including long-range scanning to obtain early warning of risk of collision and radar plotting or equivalent systematic observation of detected objects.

(c) Assumptions shall not be made on the basis of scanty information, especially scanty radar information.

(d) In determining if risk of collision exists the following considerations shall be among those taken into account:

(i) Such risk shall be deemed to exist if the compass bearing of an approaching vessel does not appreciably change.

(ii) Such risk may sometimes exist even when an appreciable bearing change is evident, particularly when approaching a very large vessel or a tow or when approaching a vessel at close range.

—INTERNATIONAL—
Steering and Sailing Rules

Rule 8
Action to Avoid Collision

(a) Any action taken to avoid collision shall be taken in accordance with the Rules of this Part and shall, if the circumstances of the case admit, be positive, made in ample time and with due regard to the observance of good seamanship.

(b) Any alteration of course and/or speed to avoid collision shall, if the circumstances of the case admit, be large enough to be readily apparent to another vessel observing visually or by radar; a succession of small alterations of course and/or speed should be avoided.

(c) If there is sufficient sea room, alteration of course alone may be the most effective action to avoid a close-quarters situation provided that it is made in good time, is substantial and does not result in another close-quarters situation.

(d) Action taken to avoid collision with another vessel shall be such as to result in passing at a safe distance. The effectiveness of the action shall be carefully checked until the other vessel is finally past and clear.

(e) If necessary to avoid collision or allow more time to assess the situation, a vessel shall slacken her speed or take all way off by stopping or reversing her means of propulsion.

(f) (i) A vessel which, by any of these rules, is required not to impede the passage or safe passage of another vessel shall, when required by the circumstances of the case, take early action to allow sufficient sea room for the safe passage of the other vessel.

(ii) A vessel required not to impede the passage or safe passage of another vessel is not relieved of this obligation if approaching the other vessel so as to involve risk of collision and shall, when taking action, have full regard to the action which may be required by the rules of this part.

(iii) A vessel, the passage of which is not to be impeded remains fully obliged to comply with the rules of this part when the two vessels are approaching one another so as to involve risk of collision.

—INLAND—
Steering and Sailing Rules

Rule 8
Action to avoid collision

§ 83.08

(a) Any action taken to avoid collision shall be taken in accordance with the Rules of this subpart (Rules 4-19) (§§ 83.04 through 83.19) and shall, if the circumstances of the case admit, be positive, made in ample time and with due regard to the observance of good seamanship.

(b) Any alteration of course and/or speed to avoid collision shall, if the circumstances of the case admit, be large enough to be readily apparent to another vessel observing visually or by radar; a succession of small alterations of course and/or speed should be avoided.

(c) If there is sufficient sea room, alteration of course alone may be the most effective action to avoid a close-quarters situation provided that it is made in good time, is substantial and does not result in another close-quarters situation.

(d) Action taken to avoid collision with another vessel shall be such as to result in passing at a safe distance. The effectiveness of the action shall be carefully checked until the other vessel is finally past and clear.

(e) If necessary to avoid collision or allow more time to assess the situation, a vessel shall slacken her speed or take all way off by stopping or reversing her means of propulsion.

(f) (i) A vessel which, by any of these Rules, is required not to impede the passage or safe passage of another vessel shall, when required by the circumstances of the case, take early action to allow sufficient sea room for the safe passage of the other vessel.

(ii) A vessel required not to impede the passage or safe passage of another vessel is not relieved of this obligation if approaching the other vessel so as to involve risk of collision and shall, when taking action, have full regard to the action which may be required by the rules of Subpart B (Rules 4-19).

(iii) A vessel the passage of which is not to be impeded remains fully obliged to comply with the Rules of Subpart B (Rules 4-19) when the two vessels are approaching one another so as to involve risk of collision.

—INTERNATIONAL—
Steering and Sailing Rules

Rule 9
Narrow Channels

(a) A vessel proceeding along the course of a narrow channel or fairway shall keep as near to the outer limit of the channel or fairway which lies on her starboard side as is safe and practicable.

(b) A vessel of less than 20 meters in length or a sailing vessel shall not impede the passage of a vessel which can safely navigate only within a narrow channel or fairway.

(c) A vessel engaged in fishing shall not impede the passage of any other vessel navigating within a narrow channel or fairway.

(d) A vessel shall not cross a narrow channel or fairway if such crossing impedes the passage of a vessel which can safely navigate only within such channel or fairway. The latter vessel may use the sound signal prescribed in Rule 34(d) if in doubt as to the intention of the crossing vessel.

(e) (i) In a narrow channel or fairway when overtaking can take place only if the vessel to be overtaken has to take action to permit safe passing, the vessel intending to overtake shall indicate her intention by sounding the appropriate signal prescribed in Rule 34(c)(i). The vessel to be overtaken shall, if in agreement, sound the appropriate signal prescribed in Rule 34(c)(ii) and take steps to permit safe passing. If in doubt she may sound the signals prescribed in Rule 34(d).

(ii) This Rule does not relieve the overtaking vessel of her obligation under Rule 13.

(f) A vessel nearing a bend or an area of a narrow channel or fairway where other vessels may be obscured by an intervening obstruction shall navigate with particular alertness and caution and shall sound the appropriate signal prescribed in Rule 34(e).

(g) Any vessel shall, if the circumstances of the case admit, avoid anchoring in a narrow channel.

—INLAND—
Steering and Sailing Rules
Rule 9
Narrow channels

§ 83.09

(a) (i) A vessel proceeding along the course of a narrow channel or fairway shall keep as near to the outer limit of the channel or fairway which lies on her starboard side as is safe and practicable.

(ii) Notwithstanding paragraph (a)(i) of this Rule and Rule 14(a) (§ 83.14(a)), a power-driven vessel operating in narrow channels or fairways on the Great Lakes, Western Rivers, or waters specified by the Secretary [‡], and proceeding downbound with a following current shall have the right-of-way over an upbound vessel, shall propose the manner and place of passage, and shall initiate the maneuvering signals prescribed by Rule 34(a)(i) (§ 83.34(a)(i)), as appropriate. The vessel proceeding upbound against the current shall hold as necessary to permit safe passing.

(b) A vessel of less than 20 meters in length or a sailing vessel shall not impede the passage of a vessel that can safely navigate only within a narrow channel or fairway.

(c) A vessel engaged in fishing shall not impede the passage of any other vessel navigating within a narrow channel or fairway.

(d) A vessel shall not cross a narrow channel or fairway if such crossing impedes the passage of a vessel which can safely navigate only within that channel or fairway. *The latter vessel shall use the signal prescribed in Rule 34(d) (§ 83.34(d)) if in doubt as to the intention of the crossing vessel.*

(e) (i) In a narrow channel or fairway when overtaking, the power-driven vessel intending to overtake another power-driven vessel shall indicate her intention by sounding the appropriate signal prescribed in Rule 34(c) (§ 83.34)(c)) and take steps to permit safe passing. The power-driven vessel being overtaken, if in agreement, shall sound the same signal and may, if specifically agreed to, take steps to permit safe passing. If in doubt she shall sound the danger signal prescribed in Rule 34(d) (§ 83.34)(d)).

(ii) This Rule does not relieve the overtaking vessel of her obligation under Rule 13 (§ 83.13).

(f) A vessel nearing a bend or an area of a narrow channel or fairway where other vessels may be obscured by an intervening obstruction shall navigate with particular alertness and caution and shall sound the appropriate signal prescribed in Rule 34(e) (§ 83.34(e)).

(g) Any vessel shall, if the circumstances of the case admit, avoid anchoring in a narrow channel.

[‡] See 33 CFR 89.25, provided for reference on page 145 of this handbook.

—INTERNATIONAL—
Steering and Sailing Rules

Rule 10
Traffic Separation Schemes

(a) This Rule applies to traffic separation schemes adopted by the Organization and does not relieve any vessel of her obligation under any other rule.

(b) A vessel using a traffic separation scheme shall:

(i) proceed in the appropriate traffic lane in the general direction of traffic flow for that lane;

(ii) so far as practicable keep clear of a traffic separation line or separation zone;

(iii) normally join or leave a traffic lane at the termination of the lane, but when joining or leaving from either side shall do so at as small an angle to the general direction of traffic flow as practicable.

(c) A vessel shall, so far as practicable, avoid crossing traffic lanes but if obliged to do so shall cross on a heading as nearly as practicable at right angles to the general direction of traffic flow.

(d) (i) A vessel shall not use an inshore traffic zone when she can safely use the appropriate traffic lane within the adjacent traffic separation scheme. However, vessels of less than 20 meters in length, sailing vessels and vessels engaged in fishing may use the inshore traffic zone.

(ii) Notwithstanding subparagraph (d)(i), a vessel may use an inshore traffic zone when en route to or from a port, offshore installation or structure, pilot station or any other place situated within the inshore traffic zone, or to avoid immediate danger.

(e) A vessel other than a crossing vessel or a vessel joining or leaving a lane shall not normally enter a separation zone or cross a separation line except:

(i) in cases of emergency to avoid immediate danger;

(ii) to engage in fishing within a separation zone.

(f) A vessel navigating in areas near the terminations of traffic separation schemes shall do so with particular caution.

(g) A vessel shall so far as practicable avoid anchoring in a traffic separation scheme or in areas near its terminations.

(h) A vessel not using a traffic separation scheme shall avoid it by as wide a margin as is practicable.

(i) A vessel engaged in fishing shall not impede the passage of any vessel following a traffic lane.

(j) A vessel of less than 20 meters in length or a sailing vessel shall not impede the safe passage of a power-driven vessel following a traffic lane.

—INLAND—
Steering and Sailing Rules

Rule 10
Traffic separation schemes

§ 83.10

(a) This Rule applies to traffic separation schemes and does not relieve any vessel of her obligation under any other Rule in subchapter E [‡].

(b) A vessel using a traffic separation scheme shall:

(i) Proceed in the appropriate traffic lane in the general direction of traffic flow for that lane;

(ii) So far as practicable keep clear of a traffic separation line or separation zone;

(iii) Normally join or leave a traffic lane at the termination of the lane, but when joining or leaving from either side shall do so at as small an angle to the general direction of traffic flow as practicable.

(c) A vessel shall, so far as practicable, avoid crossing traffic lanes but if obliged to do so shall cross on a heading as nearly as practicable at right angles to the general direction of traffic flow.

(d) (i) A vessel shall not use an inshore traffic zone when she can safely use the appropriate traffic lane within the adjacent traffic separation scheme. However, vessels of less than 20 meters in length, sailing vessels, and vessels engaged in fishing may use the inshore traffic zone.

(ii) Notwithstanding subparagraph (d)(i) of this Rule, a vessel may use an inshore traffic zone when en route to or from a port, offshore installation or structure, pilot station, or any other place situated within the inshore traffic zone, or to avoid immediate danger.

(e) A vessel other than a crossing vessel or a vessel joining or leaving a lane shall not normally enter a separation zone or cross a separation line except:

(i) In cases of emergency to avoid immediate danger;

(ii) To engage in fishing within a separation zone.

(f) A vessel navigating in areas near the terminations of traffic separation schemes shall do so with particular caution.

(g) A vessel shall so far as practicable avoid anchoring in a traffic separation scheme or in areas near its terminations.

(h) A vessel not using a traffic separation scheme shall avoid it by as wide a margin as is practicable.

(i) A vessel engaged in fishing shall not impede the passage of any vessel following a traffic lane.

(j) A vessel of less than 20 meters in length or a sailing vessel shall not impede the safe passage of a power-driven vessel following a traffic lane.

[‡] Parts 83-90 of Title 33 Code of Federal Regulations.

Rule 10—CONTINUED

(k) A vessel restricted in her ability to maneuver when engaged in an operation for the maintenance of safety of navigation in a traffic separation scheme is exempted from complying with this Rule to the extent necessary to carry out the operation.

(l) A vessel restricted in her ability to maneuver when engaged in an operation for the laying, servicing or picking up of a submarine cable, within a traffic separation scheme, is exempted from complying with this Rule to the extent necessary to carry out the operation.

Section II—Conduct of Vessels in Sight of One Another

Rule 11
Application

Rules in this section apply to vessels in sight of one another.

Rule 12
Sailing Vessels

(a) When two sailing vessels are approaching one another, so as to involve risk of collision, one of them shall keep out of the way of the other as follows:

(i) when each has the wind on a different side, the vessel which has the wind on the port side shall keep out of the way of the other;

(ii) when both have the wind on the same side, the vessel which is to windward shall keep out of the way of the vessel which is to leeward;

(iii) if a vessel with the wind on the port side sees a vessel to windward and cannot determine with certainty whether the other vessel has the wind on the port or on the starboard side, she shall keep out of the way of the other.

(b) For the purposes of this Rule the windward side shall be deemed to be the side opposite to that on which the mainsail is carried or, in the case of a square-rigged vessel, the side opposite to that on which the largest fore-and-aft sail is carried.

Rule 10—CONTINUED

(k) A vessel restricted in her ability to maneuver when engaged in an operation for the maintenance of safety of navigation in a traffic separation scheme is exempted from complying with this Rule to the extent necessary to carry out the operation.

(l) A vessel restricted in her ability to maneuver when engaged in an operation for the laying, servicing, or picking up of a submarine cable, within a traffic separation scheme, is exempted from complying with this Rule to the extent necessary to carry out the operation.

Conduct of Vessels in Sight of One Another

Rule 11
Application

§ 83.11

Rules 11 through 18 (§§ 83.11 through 83.18) apply to vessels in sight of one another.

Rule 12
Sailing vessels

§ 83.12

(a) When two sailing vessels are approaching one another, so as to involve risk of collision, one of them shall keep out of the way of the other as follows:

(i) When each has the wind on a different side, the vessel which has the wind on the port side shall keep out of the way of the other.

(ii) When both have the wind on the same side, the vessel which is to windward shall keep out of the way of the vessel which is to leeward.

(iii) If a vessel with the wind on the port side sees a vessel to windward and cannot determine with certainty whether the other vessel has the wind on the port or on the starboard side, she shall keep out of the way of the other.

(b) For the purpose of this Rule, the windward side shall be deemed to be the side opposite to that on which the mainsail is carried or, in the case of a square-rigged vessel, the side opposite to that on which the largest fore-and-aft sail is carried.

—INTERNATIONAL—
Steering and Sailing Rules

Rule 13
Overtaking

(a) Notwithstanding anything contained in the Rules of Part B, Sections I and II, any vessel overtaking any other shall keep out of the way of the vessel being overtaken.

(b) A vessel shall be deemed to be overtaking when coming up with another vessel from a direction more than 22.5° abaft her beam, that is, in such a position with reference to the vessel she is overtaking, that at night she would be able to see only the sternlight of that vessel but neither of her sidelights.

(c) When a vessel is in any doubt as to whether she is overtaking another, she shall assume that this is the case and act accordingly.

(d) Any subsequent alteration of the bearing between the two vessels shall not make the overtaking vessel a crossing vessel within the meaning of these Rules or relieve her of the duty of keeping clear of the overtaken vessel until she is finally past and clear.

Rule 14
Head-on Situation

(a) When two power-driven vessels are meeting on reciprocal or nearly reciprocal courses so as to involve risk of collision each shall alter her course to starboard so that each shall pass on the port side of the other.

(b) Such a situation shall be deemed to exist when a vessel sees the other ahead or nearly ahead and by night she could see the masthead lights of the other in a line or nearly in a line and/or both sidelights and by day she observes the corresponding aspect of the other vessel.

(c) When a vessel is in any doubt as to whether such a situation exists she shall assume that it does exist and act accordingly.

—INLAND—
Steering and Sailing Rules

Rule 13
Overtaking

§ 83.13

(a) Notwithstanding anything contained in Rules 4 through 18 (§§ 83.04 through 83.18), any vessel overtaking any other shall keep out of the way of the vessel being overtaken.

(b) A vessel shall be deemed to be overtaking when coming up with another vessel from a direction more than 22.5 degrees abaft her beam; that is, in such a position with reference to the vessel she is overtaking, that at night she would be able to see only the sternlight of that vessel but neither of her sidelights.

(c) When a vessel is in any doubt as to whether she is overtaking another, she shall assume that this is the case and act accordingly.

(d) Any subsequent alteration of the bearing between the two vessels shall not make the overtaking vessel a crossing vessel within the meaning of these Rules or relieve her of the duty of keeping clear of the overtaken vessel until she is finally past and clear.

Rule 14
Head-on situation

§ 83.14

(a) Unless otherwise agreed, when two power-driven vessels are meeting on reciprocal or nearly reciprocal courses so as to involve risk of collision each shall alter her course to starboard so that each shall pass on the port side of the other.

(b) Such a situation shall be deemed to exist when a vessel sees the other ahead or nearly ahead and by night she could see the masthead lights of the other in a line or nearly in a line and/or both sidelights and by day she observes the corresponding aspect of the other vessel.

(c) When a vessel is in any doubt as to whether such a situation exists she shall assume that it does exist and act accordingly.

(d) Notwithstanding paragraph (a) of this Rule, a power-driven vessel operating on the Great Lakes, Western Rivers, or waters specified by the Secretary [‡], and proceeding downbound with a following current shall have the right-of-way over an upbound vessel, shall propose the manner of passage, and shall initiate the maneuvering signals prescribed by Rule 34(a)(i) (§ 83.34(a)(i)), as appropriate.

[‡] See 33 CFR 89.25, provided for reference on page 145 of this handbook.

—INTERNATIONAL—
Steering and Sailing Rules

Rule 15
Crossing Situation

When two power-driven vessels are crossing so as to involve risk of collision, the vessel which has the other on her own starboard side shall keep out of the way and shall, if the circumstances of the case admit, avoid crossing ahead of the other vessel.

Rule 16
Action by Give-way Vessel

Every vessel which is directed to keep out of the way of another vessel shall, so far as possible, take early and substantial action to keep well clear.

Rule 17
Action by Stand-on Vessel

(a) (i) Where one of two vessels is to keep out of the way the other shall keep her course and speed.

(ii) The latter vessel may, however, take action to avoid collision by her maneuver alone, as soon as it becomes apparent to her that the vessel required to keep out of the way is not taking appropriate action in compliance with these Rules.

(b) When, from any cause, the vessel required to keep her course and speed finds herself so close that collision cannot be avoided by the action of the give-way vessel alone, she shall take such action as will best aid to avoid collision.

(c) A power-driven vessel which takes action in a crossing situation in accordance with subparagraph (a)(ii) of this Rule to avoid collision with another power-driven vessel shall, if the circumstances of the case admit, not alter course to port for a vessel on her own port side.

(d) This Rule does not relieve the give-way vessel of her obligation to keep out of the way.

—INLAND—
Steering and Sailing Rules

Rule 15
Crossing situation

§ 83.15

(a) When two power-driven vessels are crossing so as to involve risk of collision, the vessel which has the other on her starboard side shall keep out of the way and shall, if the circumstances of the case admit, avoid crossing ahead of the other vessel.

(b) Notwithstanding paragraph (a) of this Rule, on the Great Lakes, Western Rivers, or water specified by the Secretary [‡], a power-driven vessel crossing a river shall keep out of the way of a power-driven vessel ascending or descending the river.

Rule 16
Action by give-way vessel

§ 83.16

Every vessel which is directed to keep out of the way of another vessel shall, so far as possible, take early and substantial action to keep well clear.

Rule 17
Action by stand-on vessel

§ 83.17

(a) (i) Where one of two vessels is to keep out of the way, the other shall keep her course and speed.

(ii) The latter vessel may, however, take action to avoid collision by her maneuver alone, as soon as it becomes apparent to her that the vessel required to keep out of the way is not taking appropriate action in compliance with these Rules.

(b) When, from any cause, the vessel required to keep her course and speed finds herself so close that collision cannot be avoided by the action of the give-way vessel alone, she shall take such action as will best aid to avoid collision.

(c) A power-driven vessel which takes action in a crossing situation in accordance with paragraph (a)(ii) of this Rule to avoid collision with another power-driven vessel shall, if the circumstances of the case admit, not alter course to port for a vessel on her own port side.

(d) This Rule does not relieve the give-way vessel of her obligation to keep out of the way.

[‡] See 33 CFR 89.25, provided for reference on page 145 of this handbook.

—INTERNATIONAL—
Steering and Sailing Rules

Rule 18
Responsibilities Between Vessels

Except where Rules 9, 10 and 13 otherwise require:

(a) A power-driven vessel underway shall keep out of the way of:
  (i) a vessel not under command;
  (ii) a vessel restricted in her ability to maneuver;
  (iii) a vessel engaged in fishing;
  (iv) a sailing vessel.
(b) A sailing vessel underway shall keep out of the way of:
  (i) a vessel not under command;
  (ii) a vessel restricted in her ability to maneuver;
  (iii) a vessel engaged in fishing.
(c) A vessel engaged in fishing when underway shall, so far as possible, keep out of the way of:
  (i) a vessel not under command;
  (ii) a vessel restricted in her ability to maneuver.
(d) (i) Any vessel other than a vessel not under command or a vessel restricted in her ability to maneuver shall, if the circumstances of the case admit, avoid impeding the safe passage of a vessel constrained by her draft, exhibiting the signals in Rule 28.
  (ii) A vessel constrained by her draft shall navigate with particular caution having full regard to her special condition.
(e) A seaplane on the water shall, in general, keep well clear of all vessels and avoid impeding their navigation. In circumstances, however, where risk of collision exists, she shall comply with the Rules of this Part.

(f) (i) A WIG craft shall, when taking off, landing and in flight near the surface, keep well clear of all other vessels and avoid impeding their navigation;
  (ii) A WIG craft operating on the water surface shall comply with the Rules of this Part as a power-driven vessel.

—INLAND—
Steering and Sailing Rules

Rule 18
Responsibilities between vessels

§ 83.18

Except where Rules 9, 10, and 13 (§§ 83.09, 83.10, and 83.13) otherwise require:

(a) A power-driven vessel underway shall keep out of the way of:
    (i) A vessel not under command;
    (ii) A vessel restricted in her ability to maneuver;
    (iii) A vessel engaged in fishing;
    (iv) A sailing vessel.

(b) A sailing vessel underway shall keep out of the way of:
    (i) A vessel not under command;
    (ii) A vessel restricted in her ability to maneuver; and
    (iii) A vessel engaged in fishing.

(c) A vessel engaged in fishing when underway shall, so far as possible, keep out of the way of:
    (i) A vessel not under command; and
    (ii) A vessel restricted in her ability to maneuver.

(d) [Reserved]

(e) A seaplane on the water shall, in general, keep well clear of all vessels and avoid impeding their navigation. In circumstances, however, where risk of collision exists, she shall comply with the Rules of this Subpart (Rules 4-19) (§§ 83.04 through 83.19); and

(f) (i) a WIG craft shall, when taking off, landing and in flight near the surface, keep well clear of all other vessels and avoid impeding their navigation; and

(ii) a WIG craft operating on the water shall comply with the Rules of this Subpart (Rules 4-19) (§§ 83.04 through 83.19) as a power-driven vessel.

—INTERNATIONAL—
Steering and Sailing Rules

Section III—Conduct of Vessels in Restricted Visibility

Rule 19
Conduct of Vessels in Restricted Visibility

(a) This Rule applies to vessels not in sight of one another when navigating in or near an area of restricted visibility.

(b) Every vessel shall proceed at a safe speed adapted to the prevailing circumstances and conditions of restricted visibility. A power-driven vessel shall have her engines ready for immediate maneuver.

(c) Every vessel shall have due regard to the prevailing circumstances and conditions of restricted visibility when complying with the Rules of Section I of this part.

(d) A vessel which detects by radar alone the presence of another vessel shall determine if a close-quarters situation is developing and/or risk of collision exists. If so, she shall take avoiding action in ample time, provided that when such action consists of an alteration of course, so far as possible the following shall be avoided:

    (i) an alteration of course to port for a vessel forward of the beam, other than for a vessel being overtaken;

    (ii) an alteration of course towards a vessel abeam or abaft the beam.

(e) Except where it has been determined that a risk of collision does not exist, every vessel which hears apparently forward of her beam the fog signal of another vessel, or which cannot avoid a close-quarters situation with another vessel forward of her beam, shall reduce her speed to the minimum at which she can be kept on course. She shall if necessary take all her way off and in any event navigate *with extreme* caution until danger of collision is over.

—INLAND—
Steering and Sailing Rules

Conduct of Vessels in Restricted Visibility

Rule 19
Conduct of vessels in restricted visibility

§ 83.19

(a) This Rule applies to vessels not in sight of one another when navigating in or near an area of restricted visibility.

(b) Every vessel shall proceed at a safe speed adapted to the prevailing circumstances and conditions of restricted visibility. A power-driven vessel shall have her engines ready for immediate maneuver.

(c) Every vessel shall have due regard to the prevailing circumstances and conditions of restricted visibility when complying with Rules 4 through 10 (§§ 83.04 through 83.10).

(d) *A vessel which detects by radar alone the presence of another vessel shall determine if a close-quarters situation is developing and/or risk of collision exists.* If so, she shall take avoiding action in ample time, provided that when such action consists of an alteration of course, so far as possible the following shall be avoided:

(i) An alteration of course to port for a vessel forward of the beam, other than for a vessel being overtaken;

(ii) An alteration of course toward a vessel abeam or abaft the beam.

(e) Except where it has been determined that a risk of collision does not exist, every vessel which hears apparently forward of her beam the fog signal of another vessel, or which cannot avoid a close-quarters situation with another vessel forward of her beam, shall reduce her speed to the minimum at which she can be kept on course. She shall if necessary take all her way off and, in any event, navigate with extreme caution until danger of collision is over.

—INTERNATIONAL—
Lights and Shapes

PART C—LIGHTS AND SHAPES

Rule 20
Application

(a) Rules in this part shall be complied with in all weathers.

(b) The Rules concerning lights shall be complied with from sunset to sunrise, and during such times no other lights shall be exhibited, except such lights as cannot be mistaken for the lights specified in these Rules or do not impair their visibility or distinctive character, or interfere with the keeping of a proper look-out.

(c) The lights prescribed by these Rules shall, if carried, also be exhibited from sunrise to sunset in restricted visibility and may be exhibited in all other circumstances when it is deemed necessary.

(d) The Rules concerning shapes shall be complied with by day.

(e) The lights and shapes specified in these Rules shall comply with the provisions of Annex I to these Regulations.

—INLAND—
Lights and Shapes

SUBPART C—LIGHTS AND SHAPES

Rule 20
Application

§ 83.20

(a) Rules in this subpart (Rules 20-31) (§§ 83.20 through 83.31) shall be complied with in all weathers.

(b) The Rules concerning lights (§§ 83.20 through 83.31) shall be complied with from sunset to sunrise, and during such times no other lights shall be exhibited, except such lights as cannot be mistaken for the lights specified in these Rules or do not impair their visibility or distinctive character, or interfere with the keeping of a proper look-out.

(c) The lights prescribed by these Rules shall, if carried, also be exhibited from sunrise to sunset in restricted visibility and may be exhibited in all other circumstances when it is deemed necessary.

(d) The Rules concerning shapes shall be complied with by day.

(e) The lights and shapes specified in these Rules shall comply with the provisions of Annex I of these Rules (33 CFR Part 84).

(f) A vessel's navigation lights and shapes may be lowered if necessary to pass under a bridge.

—INTERNATIONAL—
Lights and Shapes

Rule 21
Definitions

(a) *Masthead light* means a white light placed over the fore and aft centerline of the vessel showing an unbroken light over an arc of the horizon of 225° and so fixed as to show the light from right ahead to 22.5° abaft the beam on either side of the vessel.

(b) *Sidelights* means a green light on the starboard side and a red light on the port side each showing an unbroken light over an arc of the horizon of 112.5° and so fixed as to show the light from right ahead to 22.5° abaft the beam on its respective side. In a vessel of less than 20 m in length the sidelights may be combined in one lantern carried on the fore and aft centerline of the vessel.

(c) *Sternlight* means a white light placed as nearly as practicable at the stern showing an unbroken light over an arc of the horizon of 135° and so fixed as to show the light 67.5° from right aft on each side of the vessel.

(d) *Towing light* means a yellow light having the same characteristics as the *sternlight* defined in paragraph (c) of this Rule.

(e) *All-round light* means a light showing an unbroken light over an arc of the horizon of 360°.

(f) *Flashing light* means a light flashing at regular intervals at a frequency of 120 flashes or more per minute.

—INLAND—
Lights and Shapes

Rule 21
Definitions

§ 83.21

(a) *Masthead light* means a white light placed over the fore and aft centerline of the vessel showing an unbroken light over an arc of the horizon of 225 degrees and so fixed as to show the light from right ahead to 22.5 degrees abaft the beam on either side of the vessel, except that on a vessel of less than 12 meters in length the masthead light shall be placed as nearly as practicable to the fore and aft centerline of the vessel.

(b) *Sidelights* mean a green light on the starboard side and a red light on the port side each showing an unbroken light over an arc of the horizon of 112.5 degrees and so fixed as to show the light from right ahead to 22.5 degrees abaft the beam on its respective side. On a vessel of less than 20 meters in length the sidelights may be combined in one lantern carried on the fore and aft centerline of the vessel, except that on a vessel of less than 12 meters in length the sidelights when combined in one lantern shall be placed as nearly as practicable to the fore and aft centerline of the vessel.

(c) *Sternlight* means a white light placed as nearly as practicable at the stern showing an unbroken light over an arc of the horizon of 135 degrees and so fixed as to show the light 67.5 degrees from right aft on each side of the vessel.

(d) *Towing light* means a yellow light having the same characteristics as the "sternlight" defined in paragraph (c) of this Rule.

(e) *All-round light* means a light showing an unbroken light over an arc of the horizon of 360 degrees.

(f) *Flashing light* means a light flashing at regular intervals at a frequency of 120 flashes or more per minute.

(g) *Special flashing light* means a yellow light flashing at regular intervals at a frequency of 50 to 70 flashes per minute, placed as far forward and as nearly as practicable on the fore and aft centerline of the tow and showing an unbroken light over an arc of the horizon of not less than 180 degrees nor more than 225 degrees and so fixed as to show the light from right ahead to abeam and no more than 22.5 degrees abaft the beam on either side of the vessel.

—INTERNATIONAL—
Lights and Shapes

Rule 22
Visibility of Lights

The lights prescribed in these Rules shall have an intensity as specified in Section 8 of Annex I to these Regulations so as to be visible at the following minimum ranges:

(a) In vessels of 50 meters or more in length:
  - a masthead light, 6 miles;
  - a sidelight, 3 miles;
  - a sternlight, 3 miles;
  - a towing light, 3 miles;
  - a white, red, green or yellow all-round light, 3 miles.

(b) In vessels of 12 meters or more in length but less than 50 meters in length:

  - a masthead light, 5 miles; except that where the length of the vessel is less than 20 meters, 3 miles;
  - a sidelight, 2 miles;
  - a sternlight, 2 miles;
  - a towing light, 2 miles;
  - a white, red, green or yellow all-round light, 2 miles.

(c) In vessels of less than 12 meters in length:
  - a masthead light, 2 miles;
  - a sidelight, 1 mile;
  - a sternlight, 2 miles;
  - a towing light, 2 miles;
  - a white, red, green or yellow all-round light, 2 miles.

(d) In inconspicuous, partly submerged vessels or objects being towed:
  - a white all-round light, 3 miles.

—INLAND—
Lights and Shapes

Rule 22
Visibility of lights

§ 83.22

The lights prescribed in these Rules (Subpart C) shall have an intensity as specified in Annex I to these Rules (33 CFR part 84), so as to be visible at the following minimum ranges:

(a) In a vessel of 50 meters or more in length:

(i) A masthead light, 6 miles;

(ii) A sidelight, 3 miles;

(iii) A sternlight, 3 miles;

(iv) A towing light, 3 miles;

(v) A white, red, green or yellow all-round light, 3 miles; and

(vi) A special flashing light, 2 miles.

(b) In a vessel of 12 meters or more in length but less than 50 meters in length:

(i) A masthead light, 5 miles; except that where the length of the vessel is less than 20 meters, 3 miles;

(ii) A sidelight, 2 miles;

(iii) A sternlight, 2 miles;

(iv) A towing light, 2 miles;

(v) A white, red, green or yellow all-round light, 2 miles; and

(vi) A special flashing light, 2 miles.

(c) In a vessel of less than 12 meters in length:

(i) A masthead light, 2 miles;

(ii) A sidelight, 1 mile;

(iii) A sternlight, 2 miles;

(iv) A towing light, 2 miles;

(v) A white, red, green or yellow all-round light, 2 miles; and

(vi) A special flashing light, 2 miles.

(d) In an inconspicuous, partly submerged vessel or object being towed:

(i) A white all-round light, 3 miles.

(ii) [Reserved]

—INTERNATIONAL—
Lights and Shapes

Rule 23
Power-driven Vessels Underway

(a) A power-driven vessel underway shall exhibit:
  (i) a masthead light forward;
  (ii) a second masthead light abaft of and higher than the forward one; except that a vessel of less than 50 meters in length shall not be obliged to exhibit such light but may do so;
  (iii) sidelights; and
  (iv) a sternlight.

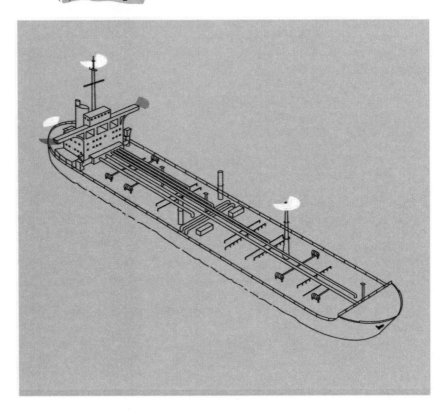

Power-driven vessel underway—50 meters or greater in length.
Same for Inland.

—INLAND—
Lights and Shapes

Rule 23
Power-driven vessels underway

§ 83.23

(a) A power-driven vessel underway shall exhibit:

(i) A masthead light forward;

(ii) A second masthead light abaft of and higher than the forward one; except that a vessel of less than 50 meters in length shall not be obliged to exhibit such light but may do so;

(iii) Sidelights; and

(iv) A sternlight.

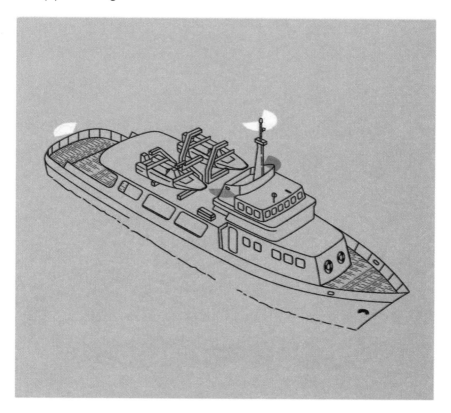

Power-driven vessel underway—less than 50 meters in length.
Same for International.

Rule 23—CONTINUED

(b) An air-cushion vessel when operating in the non-displacement mode shall, in addition to the lights prescribed in paragraph (a) of this Rule, exhibit an all-round flashing yellow light.

(c) A WIG craft only when taking off, landing and in flight near the surface shall, in addition to the lights prescribed in paragraph (a) of this Rule, exhibit a high intensity all-round flashing red light.

Air-cushion vessel when operating in the non-displacement mode— vessel less than 50 meters in length. Same for Inland.

—INLAND—
Lights and Shapes

Rule 23—CONTINUED

(b) An air-cushion vessel when operating in the non-displacement mode shall, in addition to the lights prescribed in paragraph (a) of this Rule, exhibit an all-round flashing yellow light where it can best be seen.

(c) A WIG craft only when taking off, landing and in flight near the surface shall, in addition to the lights prescribed in paragraph (a) of this Rule, exhibit a high intensity all-round _flashing_ red light.

Air-cushion vessel when operating in the <u>displacement</u> mode— vessel less than 50 meters in length. Same for International.

Rule 23—CONTINUED

(d) (i) A power-driven vessel of less than 12 meters in length may in lieu of the lights prescribed in paragraph (a) of this Rule exhibit an all-round white light and sidelights;

(ii) a power-driven vessel of less than 7 meters in length whose maximum speed does not exceed 7 knots may in lieu of the lights prescribed in paragraph (a) of this Rule exhibit an all-round white light and shall, if practicable, also exhibit sidelights;

(iii) the masthead light or all-round white light on a power-driven vessel of less than 12 meters in length may be displaced from the fore and aft centerline of the vessel if centerline fitting is not practicable, provided that the sidelights are combined in one lantern which shall be carried on the fore and aft centerline of the vessel or located as nearly as practicable in the same fore and aft line as the masthead light or the all-round white light.

Power-driven vessel of less than 7 meters in length whose maximum speed does not exceed 7 knots. International only.

—INLAND—
Lights and Shapes

Rule 23—CONTINUED

(d) A power-driven vessel of less than 12 meters in length may, in lieu of the lights prescribed in paragraph (a) of this Rule, exhibit an all-round white light and sidelights.

Power-driven vessel of less than 12 meters in length.
Same for International.

—INTERNATIONAL—
Lights and Shapes

[BLANK]

—INLAND—
Lights and Shapes

Rule 23—CONTINUED

(e) A power-driven vessel when operating on the Great Lakes may carry an all-round white light in lieu of the second masthead light and sternlight prescribed in paragraph (a) of this Rule. The light shall be carried in the position of the second masthead light and be visible at the same minimum range.

Power-driven vessel on Great Lakes.

—INTERNATIONAL—
Lights and Shapes

Rule 24
Towing and Pushing

(a) A power-driven vessel when towing shall exhibit:

(i) instead of the light prescribed in Rule 23(a)(i) or (a)(ii), two masthead lights in a vertical line. When the length of the tow, measuring from the stern of the towing vessel to the after end of the tow, exceeds 200 meters, three such lights in a vertical line;

(ii) sidelights;

(iii) a sternlight;

(iv) a towing light in a vertical line above the sternlight; and

(v) when the length of the tow exceeds 200 meters, a diamond shape where it can best be seen.

Power-driven vessel towing astern—towing vessel less than 50 meters in length; length of tow exceeds 200 meters.
Same for Inland

—INLAND—
Lights and Shapes

Rule 24
Towing and pushing

§ 83.24

(a) A power-driven vessel when towing astern shall exhibit:

(i) Instead of the light prescribed either in Rule 23(a)(i) or 23(a)(ii) (§§ 83.23(a)(i) and (ii)), two masthead lights in a vertical line. When the length of the tow, measuring from the stern of the towing vessel to the after end of the tow exceeds 200 meters, three such lights in a vertical line;

(ii) Sidelights;

(iii) A sternlight;

(iv) A towing light in a vertical line above the sternlight; and

(v) When the length of the tow exceeds 200 meters, a diamond shape where it can best be seen.

Power-driven vessel towing astern—towing vessel less than 50 meters in length; length of tow 200 meters or less.
Same for International.

Rule 24—CONTINUED

(b) When a pushing vessel and a vessel being pushed ahead are rigidly connected in a composite unit they shall be regarded as a power-driven vessel and exhibit the lights prescribed in Rule 23.

Composite unit underway.
Same for Inland.

—INLAND—
Lights and Shapes

Rule 24—CONTINUED

(b) When a pushing vessel and a vessel being pushed ahead are rigidly connected in a composite unit they shall be regarded as a power-driven vessel and exhibit the lights prescribed in Rule 23 (§ 83.23).

Composite unit underway—less than 50 meters in length.
Same for International.

—INTERNATIONAL—
Lights and Shapes

Rule 24—CONTINUED

(c) A power-driven vessel when pushing ahead or towing alongside, except in the case of a composite unit, shall exhibit:

(i) instead of the light prescribed in Rule 23(a)(i) or 23(a)(ii), two masthead lights in a vertical line;

(ii) sidelights; and

(iii) a sternlight.

Power-driven vessel pushing ahead or towing alongside—
towing vessel less than 50 meters in length.
International only.

(d) A power-driven vessel to which paragraph (a) or (c) of this Rule applies shall also comply with Rule 23(a)(ii).

Power-driven vessel towing astern—length of tow 200 meters or less. The after masthead light is optional for vessel less than 50 meters in length. Same for Inland.

—INLAND—
Lights and Shapes

Rule 24—CONTINUED

(c) A power-driven vessel when pushing ahead or towing alongside, except as required by paragraphs (b) and (i) of this Rule, shall exhibit:
 (i) Instead of the light prescribed either in Rule 23(a)(i) or 23(a)(ii) (§ 83.23)(a)(i) and (ii), two masthead lights in a vertical line;
 (ii) Sidelights; and
 (iii) Two towing lights in a vertical line.

Power-driven vessel pushing ahead or towing alongside—towing vessel less than 50 meters in length. Inland only.

(d) A power-driven vessel to which paragraphs (a) or (c) of this Rule apply shall also comply with Rule 23(a)(i) and 23(a)(ii) (§ 83.23(a)(i) or (ii)).

Power-driven vessel towing astern—length of tow 200 meters or less. When masthead lights for towing or pushing are exhibited aft, a forward masthead light is required. Same for International.

—INTERNATIONAL—
Lights and Shapes

Rule 24—CONTINUED

(e) A vessel or object being towed, other than those mentioned in paragraph (g) of this Rule, shall exhibit:
   (i) sidelights;
   (ii) a sternlight;
   (iii) when the length of the tow exceeds 200 meters, a diamond shape where it can best be seen.

Vessel or object being towed—length of tow exceeds 200 meters.
Same for Inland.

—INLAND—
Lights and Shapes

Rule 24—CONTINUED

(e) A vessel or object other than those referred to in paragraph (g) of this Rule being towed shall exhibit:
(i) Sidelights;
(ii) A sternlight; and
(iii) When the length of the tow exceeds 200 meters, a diamond shape where it can best be seen.

Vessel being towed—length of tow 200 meters or less.
Same for International.

Rule 24—CONTINUED

(f) Provided that any number of vessels being towed alongside or pushed in a group shall be lighted as one vessel:

(i) a vessel being pushed ahead, not being part of a composite unit, shall exhibit at the forward end, sidelights;

(ii) a vessel being towed alongside shall exhibit a sternlight and at the forward end, sidelights.

Vessel being pushed ahead, not being part of a composite unit.
International only.

Vessel being towed alongside.
International only.

—INLAND—
Lights and Shapes

Rule 24—CONTINUED

(f) Provided that any number of vessels being towed alongside or pushed in a group shall be lighted as one vessel, except as provided in paragraph (f)(iii) of this Rule.

(i) A vessel being pushed ahead, not being part of a composite unit, shall exhibit at the forward end, sidelights and a special flashing light.

(ii) A vessel being towed alongside shall exhibit a sternlight and at the forward end, sidelights and a special flashing light.

(iii) When vessels are towed alongside on both sides of the towing *vessel*, a sternlight shall be exhibited on the stern of the outboard vessel on each side of the towing vessel, and a single set of sidelights as far forward and as far outboard as is practicable, and a single special flashing light.

Vessel being pushed ahead, not being part of a composite unit.
Inland only.

Vessel being towed alongside. Inland only.

Rule 24—CONTINUED

(g) An inconspicuous, partly submerged vessel or object, or combination of such vessels or objects being towed, shall exhibit:

(i) if it is less than 25 meters in breadth, one all-round white light at or near the forward end and one at or near the after end except that dracones need not exhibit a light at or near the forward end;

(ii) if it is 25 meters or more in breadth, two additional all-round white lights at or near the extremities of its breadth;

(iii) if it exceeds 100 meters in length, additional all-round white lights between the lights prescribed in subparagraphs (i) and (ii) so that the distance between the lights shall not exceed 100 meters;

(iv) a diamond shape at or near the aftermost extremity of the last vessel or object being towed and if the length of the tow exceeds 200 meters an additional diamond shape where it can best be seen and located as far forward as is practicable.

(h) Where from any sufficient cause it is impracticable for a vessel or object being towed to exhibit the lights or shapes prescribed in paragraph (e) or (g) of this Rule, all possible measures shall be taken to light the vessel or object towed or at least to indicate the presence of such vessel or object.

Rule 24—CONTINUED

(g) An inconspicuous, partly submerged vessel or object, or combination of such vessels or objects being towed, shall exhibit:

(i) If it is less than 25 meters in breadth, one all-round white light at or near each end;

(ii) If it is 25 meters or more in breadth, four all-round white lights to mark its length and breadth;

(iii) If it exceeds 100 meters in length, additional all-round white lights between the lights prescribed in paragraphs (g)(i) and (ii) of this Rule so that the distance between the lights shall not exceed 100 meters: provided, that any vessels or objects being towed alongside each other shall be lighted as one vessel or object;

(iv) A diamond shape at or near the aftermost extremity of the last vessel or object being towed; and

(v) The towing vessel may direct a searchlight in the direction of the tow to indicate its presence to an approaching vessel.

(h) Where from any sufficient cause it is impracticable for a vessel or object being towed to exhibit the lights prescribed in paragraph (e) or (g) of this Rule, all possible measures shall be taken to light the vessel or object towed or at least to indicate the presence of *such* vessel or object.

Rule 24—CONTINUED

(i) Where from any sufficient cause it is impracticable for a vessel not normally engaged in towing operations to display the lights prescribed in paragraph (a) or (c) of this Rule, such vessel shall not be required to exhibit those lights when engaged in towing another vessel in distress or otherwise in need of assistance. All possible measures shall be taken to indicate the nature of the relationship between the towing vessel and the vessel being towed as authorized by Rule 36, in particular by illuminating the towline.

Rule 24—CONTINUED

(i) Notwithstanding paragraph (c) of this Rule, on the Western Rivers (except below the Huey P. Long Bridge at mile 106.1 Above Head of Passes on the Mississippi River) and on waters specified by the Secretary [‡], a power-driven vessel when pushing ahead or towing alongside, except as paragraph (b) of this Rule applies, shall exhibit:

   (i) Sidelights; and

   (ii) Two towing lights in a vertical line.

Power-driven vessel pushing ahead on Western River
(above the Huey P. Long Bridge at mile 106.1 Above Head of Passes on the Mississippi River).

(j) Where from any sufficient cause it is impracticable for a vessel not normally engaged in towing operations to display the lights prescribed by paragraph (a), (c) or (i) of this Rule, such vessel shall not be required to exhibit those lights when engaged in towing another vessel in distress or otherwise in need of assistance. All possible measures shall be taken to indicate the nature of the relationship between the towing vessel and the vessel being assisted. The searchlight authorized by Rule 36 (§ 83.36) may be used to illuminate the tow.

[‡] See 33 CFR 89.25, provided for reference on page 145 of this handbook.

—INTERNATIONAL—
Lights and Shapes

Rule 25
Sailing Vessels Underway and Vessels Under Oars

(a) A sailing vessel underway shall exhibit:
  (i) sidelights;
  (ii) a sternlight.

(b) In a sailing vessel of less than 20 meters in length the lights prescribed in paragraph (a) of this Rule may be combined in one lantern carried at or near the top of the mast where it can best be seen.

Sailing vessel underway. Same for Inland.

—INLAND—
Lights and Shapes

Rule 25
Sailing vessels underway and vessels under oars

§ 83.25

  (a) A sailing vessel underway shall exhibit:

    (i) Sidelights; and

    (ii) A sternlight.

  (b) In a sailing vessel of less than 20 meters in length the lights prescribed in paragraph (a) of this Rule may be combined in one lantern carried at or near the top of the mast where it can best be seen.

Sailing vessel underway—less than 20 meters in length.
Same for International.

—INTERNATIONAL—
Lights and Shapes

Rule 25—CONTINUED

(c) A sailing vessel underway may, in addition to the lights prescribed in paragraph (a) of this Rule, exhibit at or near the top of the mast, where they can best be seen, two all-round lights in a vertical line, the upper being red and the lower green, but these lights shall not be exhibited in conjunction with the combined lantern permitted by paragraph (b) of this Rule.

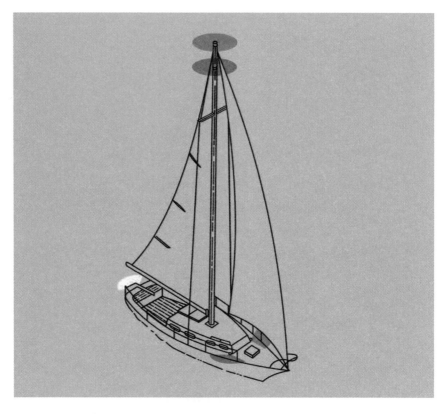

Sailing vessel underway. Same for Inland.

Rule 25—CONTINUED

(c) A sailing vessel underway may, in addition to the lights prescribed in paragraph (a) of this Rule, exhibit at or near the top of the mast, where they can best be seen, two all-round lights in a vertical line, the upper being red and the lower green, but these lights shall not be exhibited in conjunction with the combined lantern permitted by paragraph (b) of this Rule.

Rule 25—CONTINUED

(d) (i) A sailing vessel of less than 7 meters in length shall, if practicable, exhibit the lights prescribed in paragraph (a) or (b) of this Rule, but if she does not, she shall have ready at hand an electric torch or lighted lantern showing a white light which shall be exhibited in sufficient time to prevent collision.

(ii) A vessel under oars may exhibit the lights prescribed in this Rule for sailing vessels, but if she does not, she shall have ready at hand an electric torch or lighted lantern showing a white light which shall be exhibited in sufficient time to prevent collision.

Sailing vessel underway—less than 7 meters in length.
Same for Inland.

Rule 25—CONTINUED

(d) (i)A sailing vessel of less than 7 meters in length shall, if practicable, exhibit the lights prescribed in paragraph (a) or (b) of this Rule, but if she does not, she shall exhibit an all-round white light or have ready at hand an electric torch or lighted lantern showing a white light which shall be exhibited in sufficient time to prevent collision.

(ii) A vessel under oars may exhibit the lights prescribed in this Rule for sailing vessels, but if she does not, she shall exhibit an all-round white light or have ready at hand an electric torch or lighted lantern showing a white light which shall be exhibited in sufficient time to prevent collision.

Vessel under oars. Same for International.

—INTERNATIONAL—
Lights and Shapes

Rule 25—CONTINUED

(e) A vessel proceeding under sail when also being propelled by machinery shall exhibit forward where it can best be seen a conical shape, apex downwards.

Vessel proceeding under sail when also being propelled by machinery. Same for Inland except that a vessel of less than 12 meters in length is not required to exhibit the dayshape.

Rule 25—CONTINUED

(e) A vessel proceeding under sail when also being propelled by machinery shall exhibit forward where it can best be seen a conical shape, apex downward. A vessel of less than 12 meters in length is not required to exhibit this shape, but may do so.

—INTERNATIONAL—
Lights and Shapes

Rule 26
Fishing Vessels

(a) A vessel engaged in fishing, whether underway or at anchor, shall exhibit only the lights and shapes prescribed in this Rule.

(b) A vessel when engaged in trawling, by which is meant the dragging through the water of a dredge net or other apparatus used as a fishing appliance, shall exhibit:

(i) two all-round lights in a vertical line, the upper being green and the lower white, or a shape consisting of two cones with their apexes together in a vertical line one above the other;

(ii) a masthead light abaft of and higher than the all-round green light; a vessel of less than 50 meters in length shall not be obliged to exhibit such a light but may do so;

(iii) when making way through the water, in addition to the lights prescribed in this paragraph, sidelights and a sternlight.

Vessel engaged in trawling—making way; vessel less than 50 meters in length. Same for Inland.

Vessel engaged in trawling – making way; vessel over 50 meters in length. Same for Inland.

GREN OVER white
TRULLING AT night

—INLAND—
Lights and Shapes

Rule 26
Fishing vessels

§ 83.26

(a) A vessel engaged in fishing, whether underway or at anchor, shall exhibit only the lights and shapes prescribed in this Rule.

(b) A vessel when engaged in trawling, by which is meant the dragging through the water of a dredge net or other apparatus used as a fishing appliance, shall exhibit:

(i) Two all-round lights in a vertical line, the upper being green and the lower white, or a shape consisting of two cones with their apexes together in a vertical line one above the other;

(ii) A masthead light abaft of and higher than the all-round green light; a vessel of less than 50 meters in length shall not be obliged to exhibit such a light but may do so;

(iii) When making way through the water, in addition to the lights prescribed in this paragraph, sidelights and a sternlight.

Vessel engaged in trawling—not making way; vessel less than 50 meters in length. Same for International.

Vessel engaged in trawling—not making way; vessel over 50 meters in length. Same for International.

Rule 26—CONTINUED

(c) A vessel engaged in fishing, other than trawling, shall exhibit:

(i) two all-round lights in a vertical line, the upper being red and the lower white, or a shape consisting of two cones with apexes together in a vertical line one above the other;

(ii) when there is outlying gear extending more than 150 meters horizontally from the vessel, an all-round white light or a cone apex upwards in the direction of the gear;

(iii) when making way through the water, in addition to the lights prescribed in this paragraph, sidelights and a sternlight.

(d) The additional signals described in Annex II to these Rules apply to a vessel engaged in fishing in close proximity to other vessels engaged in fishing.

When there is outlying gear extending more than 150 meters horizontally from the vessel, an all-round white light or a cone apex upwards in the direction of the gear.

Vessel engaged in fishing other than trawling—making way.
Same for Inland.

red over white fishing or night

Rule 26—CONTINUED

(c) A vessel engaged in fishing, other than trawling, shall exhibit:

(i) Two all-round lights in a vertical line, the upper being red and the lower white, or a shape consisting of two cones with apexes together in a vertical line one above the other;

(ii) When there is outlying gear extending more than 150 meters horizontally from the vessel, an all-round white light or a cone apex upward in the direction of the gear; and

(iii) When making way through the water, in addition to the lights prescribed in this paragraph, sidelights and a sternlight.

(d) [Reserved]

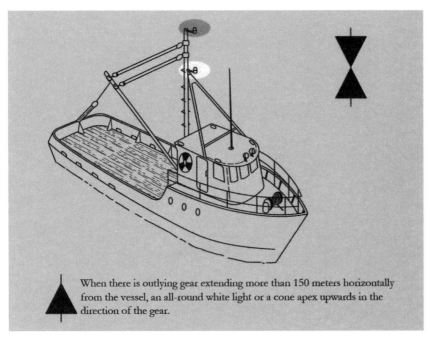

When there is outlying gear extending more than 150 meters horizontally from the vessel, an all-round white light or a cone apex upwards in the direction of the gear.

Vessel engaged in fishing other than trawling—not making way.
Same for International.

Rule 26—CONTINUED

(e) A vessel when not engaged in fishing shall not exhibit the lights or shapes prescribed in this Rule, but only those prescribed for a vessel of her length.

Rule 26—CONTINUED

(e) A vessel not engaged in fishing shall not exhibit the lights or shapes prescribed in this Rule, but only those prescribed for a vessel of her length.

(f) Additional signals for fishing vessels in close proximity:

(i) The lights mentioned herein shall be placed where they can best be seen. They shall be at least 0.9 meters apart but at a lower level than lights prescribed in this Rule. The lights shall be visible all around the horizon at a distance of at least 1 mile but at a lesser distance from the lights prescribed by these Rules for fishing vessels.

(ii) *Signals for trawlers.*

(1) Vessels when engaged in trawling, whether using demersal or pelagic gear, may exhibit:

(A) When shooting their nets: two white lights in a vertical line;

(B) When hauling their nets: one white light over one red light in a vertical line;

(C) When the net has come fast upon an obstruction: two red lights in a vertical line.

(2) Each vessel engaged in pair trawling may exhibit:

(A) By night, a searchlight directed forward and in the direction of the other vessel of the pair;

(B) When shooting or hauling their nets or when their nets have come fast upon an obstruction, the lights prescribed in paragraph (a) of this Rule.

(iii) *Signals for purse seiners.*

(1) Vessels engaged in fishing with purse seine gear may exhibit two yellow lights in a vertical line. These lights shall flash alternately every second and with equal light and occultation duration. These lights may be exhibited only when the vessel is hampered by its fishing gear.

(2) [Reserved]

—INTERNATIONAL—
Lights and Shapes

Rule 27
Vessels Not Under Command or Restricted in Their Ability to Maneuver

(a) A vessel not under command shall exhibit:
    (i) two all-round red lights in a vertical line where they can best be seen;
    (ii) two balls or similar shapes in a vertical line where they can best be seen;
    (iii) when making way through the water, in addition to the lights prescribed in this paragraph, sidelights and a sternlight.

Vessel not under command—not making way. Same for Inland.

red over Red captains
red d

—INLAND—
Lights and Shapes

Rule 27
Vessels not under command or restricted in their ability to maneuver

§ 83.27

(a) A vessel not under command shall exhibit:

(i) Two all-round red lights in a vertical line where they can best be seen;

(ii) Two balls or similar shapes in a vertical line where they can best be seen; and

(iii) When making way through the water, in addition to the lights prescribed in this paragraph, sidelights and a sternlight.

Vessel not under command—making way. Same for International.

Rule 27—CONTINUED

(b) A vessel restricted in her ability to maneuver, except a vessel engaged in mine clearance operations, shall exhibit:

(i) three all-round lights in a vertical line where they can best be seen. The highest and lowest of these lights shall be red and the middle light shall be white;

(ii) three shapes in a vertical line where they can best be seen. The highest and lowest of these shapes shall be balls and the middle one a diamond;

(iii) when making way through the water, a masthead light or lights, sidelights and a sternlight, in addition to the lights prescribed in subparagraph (i);

(iv) when at anchor, in addition to the lights or shapes prescribed in subparagraphs (i) and (ii), the light, lights or shape prescribed in Rule 30.

Vessel restricted in her ability to maneuver—making way; vessel less than 50 meters in length. Same for Inland.

—INLAND—
Lights and Shapes

Rule 27—CONTINUED

(b) A vessel restricted in her ability to maneuver, except a vessel engaged in mine clearance operations, shall exhibit:

(i) Three all-round lights in a vertical line where they can best be seen. The highest and lowest of these lights shall be red and the middle light shall be white;

(ii) Three shapes in a vertical line where they can best be seen. The highest and lowest of these shapes shall be balls and the middle one a diamond;

(iii) When making way through the water, a masthead light or lights, sidelights and a sternlight, in addition to the lights prescribed in paragraph (b)(i) of this Rule; and

(iv) When at anchor, in addition to the lights or shapes prescribed in paragraphs (b)(i) and (ii), the light, lights or shapes prescribed in Rule 30 (§ 83.30).

Vessel restricted in her ability to maneuver—at anchor; vessel less than 50 meters in length. Same for International.

Rule 27—CONTINUED

(c) A power-driven vessel engaged in a towing operation such as severely restricts the towing vessel and her tow in their ability to deviate from their course shall, in addition to the lights or shapes prescribed in Rule 24(a), exhibit the lights or shapes prescribed in subparagraphs (b)(i) and (ii) of this Rule.

—INLAND—
Lights and Shapes

Rule 27—CONTINUED

(c) A vessel engaged in a towing operation which severely restricts the towing vessel and her tow in their ability to deviate from their course shall, in addition to the lights or shapes prescribed in subparagraphs (b)(i) and (ii) of this Rule, exhibit the lights or shape prescribed in Rule 24 (§ 83.24).

Vessel engaged in towing operation which severely restricts towing vessel and her tow in their ability to deviate from their course—length of tow does not exceed 200 meters; towing vessel less than 50 meters in length.
Same for International.

—INTERNATIONAL—
Lights and Shapes

Rule 27—CONTINUED

(d) A vessel engaged in dredging or underwater operations, when restricted in her ability to maneuver, shall exhibit the lights and shapes prescribed in subparagraphs (b)(i), (ii) and (iii) of this Rule and shall in addition, when an obstruction exists, exhibit:

(i) two all-round red lights or two balls in a vertical line to indicate the side on which the obstruction exists;

(ii) two all-round green lights or two diamonds in a vertical line to indicate the side on which another vessel may pass;

(iii) when at anchor, the lights or shapes prescribed in this paragraph instead of the lights or shape prescribed in Rule 30.

Vessel engaged in dredging or underwater operations when restricted in ability to maneuver—making way with an obstruction on the starboard side. Same for Inland.

Vessel engaged in dredging or underwater operations when restricted in ability to maneuver—not making way with an obstruction on the starboard side. Same for Inland.

Rule 27—CONTINUED

(d) A vessel engaged in dredging or underwater operations, when restricted in her ability to maneuver, shall exhibit the lights and shapes prescribed in subparagraphs (b)(i), (ii), and (iii) of this Rule and shall in addition, when an obstruction exists, exhibit:

(i) Two all-round red lights or two balls in a vertical line to indicate the side on which the obstruction exists;

(ii) Two all-round green lights or two diamonds in a vertical line to indicate the side on which another vessel may pass; and

(iii) When at anchor, the lights or shape prescribed by this paragraph, instead of the lights or shape prescribed in Rule 30 (§ 83.30).

(iv) Dredge pipelines that are floating or supported on trestles shall display the following lights at night and in periods of restricted visibility.

(1) One row of yellow lights. The lights must be:

(A) Flashing 50 to 70 times per minute,

(B) Visible all around the horizon,

(C) Visible for at least 2 miles,

(D) Not less than 1 and not more than 3.5 meters above the water,

(E) Approximately equally spaced, and

(F) Not more than 10 meters apart where the pipeline crosses a navigable channel. Where the pipeline does not cross a navigable channel the lights must be sufficient in number to clearly show the pipeline's length and course.

(2) Two red lights at each end of the pipeline, including the ends in a channel where the pipeline is separated to allow vessels to pass (whether open or closed). The lights must be:

(A) Visible all around the horizon, and

(B) Visible for at least 2 miles, and

(C) One meter apart in a vertical line with the lower light at the same height above the water as the flashing yellow light.

Rule 27—CONTINUED

(e) Whenever the size of a vessel engaged in diving operations makes it impracticable to exhibit all lights and shapes prescribed in paragraph (d) of this Rule, the following shall be exhibited:

(i) three all-round lights in a vertical line where they can best be seen. The highest and lowest of these lights shall be red and the middle light shall be white;

(ii) a rigid replica of the International Code flag "A" not less than 1 meter in height. Measures shall be taken to ensure its all-round visibility.

Small vessel engaged in diving operations by day.
Same for Inland.

Rule 27—CONTINUED

(e) Whenever the size of a vessel engaged in diving operations makes it impracticable to exhibit all lights and shapes prescribed in paragraph (d) of this Rule, as appropriate, the following shall instead be exhibited:

(i) Three all-round lights in a vertical line where they can best be seen. The highest and lowest of these lights shall be red and the middle light shall be white;

(ii) A rigid replica of the International Code flag "A" not less than 1 meter in height. Measures shall be taken to ensure its all-round visibility.

Small vessel engaged in diving operations at night or in restricted visibility.
Same for International.

Rule 27—CONTINUED

(f) A vessel engaged in mine clearance operations shall, in addition to the lights prescribed for a power-driven vessel in Rule 23 or to the lights or shape prescribed for a vessel at anchor in Rule 30 as appropriate, exhibit three all-round green lights or three balls. One of these lights or shapes shall be exhibited near the foremast head and one at each end of the fore yard. These lights or shapes indicate that it is dangerous for another vessel to approach within 1000 meters of the mine clearance vessel.

Vessel engaged in mine clearance operations—vessel less than 50 meters in length. Same for Inland.

(g) Vessels of less than 12 meters in length, except those engaged in diving operations, shall not be required to exhibit the lights and shapes prescribed in this Rule.

(h) The signals prescribed in this Rule are not signals of vessels in distress and requiring assistance. Such signals are contained in Annex IV to these Regulations.

Rule 27—CONTINUED

(f) A vessel engaged in mine clearance operations shall, in addition to the lights prescribed for a power-driven vessel in Rule 23 (§ 83.23) or to the lights or shape prescribed for a vessel at anchor in Rule 30 (§ 83.30), as appropriate, exhibit three all-round green lights or three balls. One of these lights or shapes shall be exhibited near the foremast head and one at each end of the fore yard. These lights or shapes indicate that it is dangerous for another vessel to approach within 1000 meters of the mine clearance vessel.

Vessel engaged in mine clearance operations.
Same for International.

(g) A vessel of less than 12 meters in length, except when engaged in diving operations, is not required to exhibit the lights or shapes prescribed in this Rule.

(h) The signals prescribed in this Rule are not signals of vessels in distress and requiring assistance. Such signals are contained in Annex IV to these Rules (33 CFR part 87).

—INTERNATIONAL—
Lights and Shapes

Vessels Constrained by Their Draft

A vessel constrained by her draft may, in addition to the lights prescribed for power-driven vessels in Rule 23, exhibit where they can best be seen three all-round red lights in a vertical line, or a cylinder.

Vessel constrained by her draft—underway –
50 meters or greater in length.

—INLAND—
Lights and Shapes

Rule 28

[Reserved]

—INTERNATIONAL—
Lights and Shapes

Rule 29
Pilot Vessels

(a) A vessel engaged on pilotage duty shall exhibit:

(i) at or near the masthead, two all-round lights in a vertical line, the upper being white and the lower red;

(ii) when underway, in addition, sidelights and a sternlight;

(iii) when at anchor, in addition to the lights prescribed in subparagraph (i), the anchor light, lights, or shape prescribed in Rule 30 for vessels at anchor.

(b) A pilot vessel when not engaged on pilotage duty shall exhibit the lights or shapes prescribed for a similar vessel of her length.

Vessel engaged on pilotage duty—underway.
Same for Inland.

—INLAND—
Lights and Shapes

Rule 29
Pilot vessels

§ 83.29

(a) A vessel engaged on pilotage duty shall exhibit:

(i) At or near the masthead, two all-round lights in a vertical line, the upper being white and the lower red;

(ii) When underway, in addition, sidelights and a sternlight; and

(iii) *When at anchor, in addition to the lights prescribed in subparagraph (i) of this Rule, the anchor light, lights, or shape prescribed in Rule 30 (§ 83.30) for vessels at anchor.*

(b) A pilot vessel when not engaged on pilotage duty shall exhibit the lights or shapes prescribed for a vessel of her length.

Vessel engaged on pilotage duty—at anchor; vessel of less than 50 meters in length. Same for International.

—INTERNATIONAL—
Lights and Shapes

Rule 30
Anchored Vessels and Vessels Aground

(a) A vessel at anchor shall exhibit where it can best be seen:
 (i) in the fore part, an all-round white light or one ball;
 (ii) at or near the stern and at a lower level than the light prescribed in subparagraph (i), an all-round white light.

(b) A vessel of less than 50 meters in length may exhibit an all-round white light where it can best be seen instead of the lights prescribed in paragraph (a) of this Rule.

(c) A vessel at anchor may, and a vessel of 100 meters and more in length shall, also use the available working or equivalent lights to illuminate her decks.

Vessel at anchor—less than 50 meters in length.
Same for Inland.

—INLAND—
Lights and Shapes

Rule 30
Vessels anchored, aground and moored barges
§ 83.30

(a) A vessel at anchor shall exhibit where it can best be seen:

(i) In the fore part, an all-round white light or one ball;

(ii) At or near the stern and at a lower level than the light prescribed in paragraph (i) of this Rule, an all-round white light.

(b) A vessel of less than 50 meters in length may exhibit an all-round white light where it can best be seen instead of the lights prescribed in paragraph (a) of this Rule.

(c) A vessel at anchor may, and a vessel of 100 meters or more in length shall, also use the available working or equivalent lights to illuminate her decks.

Vessel at anchor with deck illumination.
Same for International.

Rule 30—CONTINUED

(d) A vessel aground shall exhibit the lights prescribed in paragraph (a) or (b) of this Rule and in addition, where they can best be seen:
  (i) two all-round red lights in a vertical line;
  (ii) three balls in a vertical line.

Vessel aground. Same for Inland.

(e) A vessel of less than 7 meters in length, when at anchor, not in or near a narrow channel, fairway or anchorage, or where other vessels normally navigate, shall not be required to exhibit the lights or shape prescribed in paragraphs (a) and (b) of this Rule.

(f) A vessel of less than 12 meters in length, when aground, shall not be required to exhibit the lights or shapes prescribed in subparagraphs (d)(i) and (ii) of this Rule.

Rule 30—CONTINUED

(d) A vessel aground shall exhibit the lights prescribed in paragraph (a) or (b) of this Rule and in addition, if practicable, where they can best be seen:
  (i) Two all-round red lights in a vertical line; and
  (ii) Three balls in a vertical line.

Vessel aground—less than 50 meters in length.
Same for International.

(e) A vessel of less than 7 meters in length, when at anchor, not in or near a narrow channel, fairway, anchorage, or where other vessels normally navigate, shall not be required to exhibit the lights or shape prescribed in paragraphs (a) and (b) of this Rule.

(f) A vessel of less than 12 meters in length when aground shall not be required to exhibit the lights or shapes prescribed in paragraphs (d)(i) and (ii) of this Rule.

(g) A vessel of less than 20 meters in length, when at anchor in a special anchorage area designated by the Coast Guard [‡], shall not be required to exhibit the anchor lights and shapes required by this Rule.

(h) The following barges shall display at night and if practicable in periods of restricted visibility the lights described in paragraph (i) of this Rule:
  (i) Every barge projecting into a buoyed or restricted channel.
  (ii) Every barge so moored that it reduces the available navigable width of any channel to less than 80 meters.
  (iii) Barges moored in groups more than two barges wide or to a maximum width of over 25 meters.
  (iv) Every barge not moored parallel to the bank or dock.

[‡] See 33 CFR 110 Subpart A

—INTERNATIONAL—
Lights and Shapes

[BLANK]

Rule 30—CONTINUED

(i)Barges described in paragraph (h) of this Rule shall carry two unobstructed all-round white lights of an intensity to be visible for at least 1 nautical mile and meeting the technical requirements as prescribed in Annex I (33 CFR part 84).

(j)A barge or a group of barges at anchor or made fast to one or more mooring buoys or other similar device, in lieu of the provisions of this Rule, may carry unobstructed all-round white lights of an intensity to be visible for at least 1 nautical mile that meet the requirements of Annex I (33 CFR part 84) and shall be arranged as follows:

(i) Any barge that projects from a group formation, shall be lighted on its outboard corners.

(ii)On a single barge moored in water where other vessels normally navigate on both sides of the barge, lights shall be placed to mark the corner extremities of the barge.

(iii) On barges moored in group formation, moored in water where other vessels normally navigate on both sides of the group, lights shall be placed to mark the corner extremities of the group.

(k)The following are exempt from the requirements of this Rule:

(i) A barge or group of barges moored in a slip or slough used primarily for mooring purposes.

(ii)A barge or group of barges moored behind a pierhead.

(iii) A barge less than 20 meters in length when moored in a special anchorage area designated in accordance with § 109.10 of this chapter.

(l)Barges moored in well-illuminated areas are exempt from the lighting requirements of this *Rule*. These areas are as follows:

CHICAGO SANITARY
SHIP CANAL
(1) Mile 293.2 to 293.9
(2) Mile 295.2 to 296.1
(3) Mile 297.5 to 297.8
(4) Mile 298 to 298.2
(5) Mile 298.6 to 298.8
(6) Mile 299.3 to 299.4
(7) Mile 299.8 to 300.5
(8) Mile 303 to 303.2
(9) Mile 303.7 to 303.9
(10) Mile 305.7 to 305.8
(11) Mile 310.7 to 310.9
(12) Mile 311 to 311.2
(13) Mile 312.5 to 312.6
(14) Mile 313.8 to 314.2
(15) Mile 314.6
(16) Mile 314.8 to 315.3
(17) Mile 315.7 to 316
(18) Mile 316.8

(19) Mile 316.85 to
317.05
(20) Mile 317.5
(21) Mile 318.4 to 318.9
(22) Mile 318.7 to 318.8
(23) Mile 320 to 320.3
(24) Mile 320.6
(25) Mile 322.3.6 to
322.4
(26) Mile 322.8
(27) Mile 322.9 to 327.2

CALUMET SAG
CHANNEL
(28) Mile 316.5

LITTLE CALUMET
RIVER
(29) Mile 321.2
(30) Mile 322.3

CALUMET RIVER
(31) Mile 328.5 to 328.7
(32) Mile 329.2 to 329.4
(33) Mile 330 west bank
to 330.2
(34) Mile 331.4 to 331.6
(35) Mile 332.2 to 332.4
(36) Mile 332.6 to 332.8

CUMBERLAND RIVER
(37) Mile 126.8
(38) Mile 191

—INTERNATIONAL—
Lights and Shapes

Rule 31
Seaplanes

Where it is impracticable for a seaplane or a WIG craft to exhibit lights and shapes of the characteristics or in the positions prescribed in the Rules of this Part she shall exhibit lights and shapes as closely similar in characteristics and position as is possible.

PART D—SOUND AND LIGHT SIGNALS

Rule 32
Definitions

(a) The word *whistle* means any sound signaling appliance capable of producing the prescribed blasts and which complies with the specifications in Annex III to these Regulations.

(b) The term *short blast* means a blast of about one second's duration.

(c) The term *prolonged blast* means a blast of from four to six seconds' duration.

Rule 33
Equipment for Sound Signals

(a) A vessel of 12 meters or more in length shall be provided with a whistle, a vessel of 20 meters or more in length shall be provided with a bell in addition to a whistle, and a vessel of 100 meters or more in length shall, in addition, be provided with a gong, the tone and sound of which cannot be confused with that of the bell. The whistle, bell and gong shall comply with the specifications in Annex III to these Regulations. The bell or gong or both may be replaced by other equipment having the same respective sound characteristics, provided that manual sounding of the prescribed signals shall always be possible.

(b) A vessel of less than 12 meters in length shall not be obliged to carry the sound signaling appliances prescribed in paragraph (a) of this Rule but if she does not, she shall be provided with some other means of making an efficient sound signal.

—INLAND—
Lights and Shapes

Rule 31
Seaplanes

§ 83.31

Where it is impracticable for a seaplane or a WIG craft to exhibit lights and shapes of the characteristics or in the positions prescribed in the Rules of this subpart, she shall exhibit lights and shapes as closely similar in characteristics and position as is possible.

SUBPART D—SOUND AND LIGHT SIGNALS

Rule 32
Definitions

§ 83.32

(a) The word *whistle* means any sound signaling appliance capable of producing the prescribed blasts and which complies with specifications in Annex III to these Rules (33 CFR part 86).

(b) The term *short blast* means a blast of about 1 second's duration.

(c) The term *prolonged blast* means a blast of from 4 to 6 seconds' duration.

Rule 33
Equipment for Sound Signals

§ 83.33

(a) A vessel of 12 meters or more in length shall be provided with a whistle, a vessel of 20 meters or more in length shall be provided with a bell in addition to a whistle, and a vessel of 100 meters or more in length shall, in addition, be provided with a gong, the tone and sound of which cannot be confused with that of the bell. The whistle, bell and gong shall comply with the specifications in Annex III to these Rules (33 CFR part 86). The bell or gong or both may be replaced by other equipment having the same respective sound characteristics, provided that manual sounding of the prescribed signals shall always be possible.

(b) A vessel of less than 12 meters in length shall not be obliged to carry the sound signaling appliances prescribed in paragraph (a) of this Rule but if she does not, she shall be provided with some other means of making an efficient sound signal.

—INTERNATIONAL—
Sound and Light Signals

Rule 34
Maneuvering and Warning Signals

(a) When vessels are in sight of one another, a power-driven vessel underway, when maneuvering as authorized or required by these Rules, shall indicate that maneuver by the following signals on her whistle:

- one short blast to mean "I am altering my course to starboard";

- two short blasts to mean "I am altering my course to port";

- three short blasts to mean "I am operating astern propulsion".

(b) Any vessel may supplement the whistle signals prescribed in paragraph (a) of this Rule by light signals, repeated as appropriate, while the maneuver is being carried out:
(i) these light signals shall have the following significance:
- one flash to mean "I am altering my course to starboard";
- two flashes to mean "I am altering my course to port";
- three flashes to mean "I am operating astern propulsion";
(ii) the duration of each flash shall be about one second, the interval between flashes shall be about one second, and the interval between successive signals shall be not less than ten seconds;
(iii) the light used for this signal shall, if fitted, be an all-round white light, visible at a minimum range of 5 miles, and shall comply with the provisions of Annex I to these Regulations.

(c) When in sight of one another in a narrow channel or fairway:
(i) a vessel intending to overtake another shall in compliance with Rule 9(e)(i) indicate her intention by the following signals on her whistle:
- two prolonged blasts followed by one short blast to mean "I intend to overtake you on your starboard side";
- two prolonged blasts followed by two short blasts to mean "I intend to overtake you on your port side".
(ii) the vessel about to be overtaken when acting in accordance with Rule 9(e)(i) shall indicate her agreement by the following signal on her whistle:
- one prolonged, one short, one prolonged and one short blast, in that order.

DISAGREE FIVE SHORT

98

—INLAND—
Sound and Light Signals

Rule 34
Maneuvering and Warning Signals

§ 83.34

(a) When power-driven vessels are in sight of one another and meeting or crossing at a distance within half a mile of each other, each vessel underway, when maneuvering as authorized or required by these Rules:

    (i) Shall indicate that maneuver by the following signals on her whistle:

        (1) One short blast to mean "I intend to leave you on my port side";

        (2) Two short blasts to mean "I intend to leave you on my starboard side"; and

        (3) Three short blasts to mean "I am operating astern propulsion".

    (ii) Upon hearing the one or two blast signal of the other shall, if in agreement, sound the same whistle signal and take the steps necessary to effect a safe passing. If, however, from any cause, the vessel doubts the safety of the proposed maneuver, she shall sound the *danger** signal specified in paragraph (d) of this Rule and each vessel shall take appropriate precautionary action until a safe passing agreement is made.

(b) A vessel may supplement the whistle signals prescribed in paragraph (a) of this Rule by light signals:

    (i) These signals shall have the following significance:

        (1) One flash to mean "I intend to leave you on my port side";

        (2) Two flashes to mean "I intend to leave you on my starboard side";

        (3) Three flashes to mean "I am operating astern propulsion";

    (ii) The duration of each flash shall be about 1 second; and

    (iii) The light used for this signal shall, if fitted, be one all-round white or yellow light, visible at a minimum range of 2 miles, synchronized with the whistle, and shall comply with the provisions of Annex I to these Rules (33 CFR part 84).

(c) When in sight of one another:

    (i) A power-driven vessel intending to overtake another power-driven vessel shall indicate her intention by the following signals on her whistle:

        (1) One short blast to mean "I intend to overtake you on your starboard side";

        (2) Two short blasts to mean "I intend to overtake you on your port side"; and

    (ii) The power-driven vessel about to be overtaken shall, if in agreement, sound a similar sound signal. If in doubt she shall sound the *danger** signal prescribed in paragraph (d) of this Rule.

FIVE SHORT

* Prior to this reprint Paradise Cay Publications was made aware that the word "danger" which appears two times on this page may be deleted. If this change is approved it will appear in a notice to mariners announcement which can be found here: paracay.com/ntm .Please monitor this link to keep your Navigation Rules book up-to-date.

Rule 34—CONTINUED

(d) When vessels in sight of one another are approaching each other and from any cause either vessel fails to understand the intentions or actions of the other, or is in doubt whether sufficient action is being taken by the other to avoid collision, the vessel in doubt shall immediately indicate such doubt by giving at least five short and rapid blasts on the whistle. *Such signal may be supplemented by a light signal of at least five short and rapid flashes.*

(e) A vessel nearing a bend or an area of a channel or fairway where other vessels may be obscured by an intervening obstruction shall sound one prolonged blast. Such signal shall be answered with a prolonged blast by any approaching vessel that may be within hearing around the bend or behind the intervening obstruction.

(f) If whistles are fitted on a vessel at a distance apart of more than 100 meters, one whistle only shall be used for giving maneuvering and warning signals.

Rule 34—CONTINUED

(d) When vessels in sight of one another are approaching each other and, from any cause, either vessel fails to understand the intentions or actions of the other, or is in doubt whether sufficient action is being taken by the other to avoid collision, the vessel in doubt shall immediately indicate such doubt by giving at least five short and rapid blasts on the whistle. _Such signal may be supplemented by a light signal of at least five short and rapid flashes._

(e) A vessel nearing a bend or an area of a channel or fairway where other vessels may be obscured by an intervening obstruction shall sound one prolonged blast. This signal shall be answered with a prolonged blast by any approaching vessel that may be within hearing around the bend or behind the intervening obstruction.

(f) If whistles are fitted on a vessel at a distance apart of more than 100 meters, one whistle only shall be used for giving maneuvering and warning signals.

(g) When a power-driven vessel is leaving a dock or berth, she shall sound one prolonged blast.

(h) A vessel that reaches agreement with another vessel in a head-on, crossing, or overtaking situation, as for example, by using the radiotelephone as prescribed by the Vessel Bridge-to-Bridge Radiotelephone Act (85 Stat. 164; 33 U.S.C. 1201 _et seq._), is not obliged to sound the whistle signals prescribed by this Rule, but may do so. If agreement is not reached, then whistle signals shall be exchanged in a timely manner and shall prevail.

—INTERNATIONAL—
Sound and Light Signals

Rule 35
Sound Signals in Restricted Visibility

In or near an area of restricted visibility, whether by day or night, the signals prescribed in this Rule shall be used as follows:

(a) A power-driven vessel making way through the water shall sound at intervals of not more than 2 minutes one prolonged blast.

(b) A power-driven vessel underway but stopped and making no way through the water shall sound at intervals of not more than 2 minutes two prolonged blasts in succession with an interval of about 2 seconds between them.

(c) A vessel not under command, a vessel restricted in her ability to maneuver, a vessel constrained by her draft, a sailing vessel, a vessel engaged in fishing and a vessel engaged in towing or pushing another vessel shall, instead of the signals prescribed in paragraphs (a) or (b) of this Rule, sound at intervals of not more than 2 minutes three blasts in succession, namely one prolonged followed by two short blasts.

(d) A vessel engaged in fishing, when at anchor, and a vessel restricted in her ability to maneuver when carrying out her work at anchor, shall instead of the signals prescribed in paragraph (g) of this Rule sound the signal prescribed in paragraph (c) of this Rule.

(e) A vessel towed or if more than one vessel is towed the last vessel of the tow, if manned, shall at intervals of not more than 2 minutes sound four blasts in succession, namely one prolonged followed by three short blasts. When practicable, this signal shall be made immediately after the signal made by the towing vessel.

(f) When a pushing vessel and a vessel being pushed ahead are rigidly connected in a composite unit they shall be regarded as a power-driven vessel and shall give the signals prescribed in paragraphs (a) or (b) of this Rule.

—INLAND—
Sound and Light Signals

Rule 35
Sound Signals in Restricted Visibility

§ 83.35

In or near an area of restricted visibility, whether by day or night, the signals prescribed in this Rule shall be used as follows:

(a) A power-driven vessel making way through the water shall sound at intervals of not more than 2 minutes, one prolonged blast.

(b) A power-driven vessel underway but stopped and making no way through the water shall sound, at intervals of not more than 2 minutes, two prolonged blasts in succession, with an interval of about 2 seconds between them.

(c) A vessel not under command; a vessel restricted in her ability to maneuver, whether underway or at anchor; a sailing vessel; a vessel engaged in fishing, whether underway or at anchor; and a vessel engaged in towing or pushing another vessel shall, instead of the signals prescribed in paragraphs (a) or (b) of this Rule, sound at intervals of not more than 2 minutes, three blasts in succession, namely, one prolonged followed by two short blasts.

(d) [Reserved]

(e) A vessel towed or if more than one vessel is towed the last vessel of the tow, if manned, shall at intervals of not more than 2 minutes sound four blasts in succession, namely, one prolonged followed by three short blasts. When practicable, this signal shall be made immediately after the signal made by the towing vessel.

(f) When a pushing vessel and a vessel being pushed ahead are rigidly connected in a composite unit they shall be regarded as a power-driven vessel and shall give the signals prescribed in paragraphs (a) or (b) of this Rule.

Rule 35—CONTINUED

(g) A vessel at anchor shall at intervals of not more than one minute ring the bell rapidly for about 5 seconds. In a vessel of 100 meters or more in length the bell shall be sounded in the forepart of the vessel and immediately after the ringing of the bell the gong shall be sounded rapidly for about 5 seconds in the after part of the vessel. A vessel at anchor may in addition sound three blasts in succession, namely one short, one prolonged and one short blast, to give warning of her position and of the possibility of collision to an approaching vessel.

(h) A vessel aground shall give the bell signal and if required the gong signal prescribed in paragraph (g) of this Rule and shall, in addition, give three separate and distinct strokes on the bell immediately before and after the rapid ringing of the bell. A vessel aground may in addition sound an appropriate whistle signal.

(i) A vessel of 12 meters or more but less than 20 meters in length shall not be obliged to give the bell signals prescribed in paragraphs (g) and (h) of this Rule. However, if she does not, she shall make some other efficient sound signal at intervals of not more than 2 minutes.

(j) A vessel of less than 12 meters in length shall not be obliged to give the above-mentioned signals but, if she does not, shall make some other efficient sound signal at intervals of not more than 2 minutes.

(k) A pilot vessel when engaged on pilotage duty may in addition to the signals prescribed in paragraphs (a), (b) or (g) of this Rule sound an identity signal consisting of four short blasts.

Rule 36
Signals to Attract Attention

If necessary to attract the attention of another vessel, any vessel may make light or sound signals that cannot be mistaken for any signal authorized elsewhere in these Rules, or may direct the beam of her searchlight in the direction of the danger, in such a way as not to embarrass any vessel. Any light to attract the attention of another vessel shall be such that it cannot be mistaken for any aid to navigation. For the purpose of this Rule the use of high intensity intermittent or revolving lights, such as strobe lights, shall be avoided.

—INLAND—
Sound and Light Signals

Rule 35—CONTINUED

(g) A vessel at anchor shall at intervals of not more than 1 minute ring the bell rapidly for about 5 seconds. In a vessel of 100 meters or more in length the bell shall be sounded in the forepart of the vessel and immediately after the ringing of the bell the gong shall be sounded rapidly for about 5 seconds in the after part of the vessel. A vessel at anchor may in addition sound three blasts in succession, namely, one short, one prolonged and one short blast, to give warning of her position and of the possibility of collision to an approaching vessel.

(h) A vessel aground shall give the bell signal and if required the gong signal prescribed in paragraph (g) of this Rule and shall, in addition, give three separate and distinct strokes on the bell immediately before and after the rapid ringing of the bell. A vessel aground may in addition sound an appropriate whistle signal.

(i) A vessel of 12 meters or more but less than 20 meters in length shall not be obliged to give the bell signals prescribed in paragraphs (g) and (h) of this Rule. However, if she does not, she shall make some other efficient sound signal at intervals of not more than 2 minutes.

(j) A vessel of less than 12 meters in length shall not be obliged to give the bell signals prescribed in paragraphs (g) and (h) of this Rule. However, if she does not, shall make some other efficient sound signal at intervals of not more than 2 minutes.

(k) A pilot vessel when engaged on pilotage duty may, in addition to the signals prescribed in paragraphs (a), (b) or (g) of this Rule, sound an identity signal consisting of four short blasts.

(l) The following vessels shall not be required to sound signals as prescribed in paragraph (g) of this Rule when anchored in a special anchorage area designated by the Coast Guard:

    (i) A vessel of less than 20 meters in length; and

    (ii) A barge, canal boat, scow, or other nondescript craft.

Rule 36
Signals to Attract Attention

§ 83.36

If necessary to attract the attention of another vessel, any vessel may make light or sound signals that cannot be mistaken for any signal authorized elsewhere in these Rules, or may direct the beam of her searchlight in the direction of the danger, in such a way as not to embarrass any vessel.

—INTERNATIONAL—
Sound and Light Signals

Rule 37
Distress Signals

When a vessel is in distress and requires assistance she shall use or exhibit the signals described in Annex IV to these Regulations.

DISTRESS SIGNALS
72 COLREGS

RED STAR SHELLS

FOG HORN CONTINUOUS SOUNDING

FLAMES ON A VESSEL

GUN FIRED AT INTERVALS OF 1 MIN.

ORANGE BACKGROUND BLACK BALL AND SQUARE

SOS SOS

"MAYDAY" BY RADIO

PARACHUTE RED FLARE

DYE MARKER (ANY COLOR)

CODE FLAGS NOVEMBER CHARLIE

SQUARE FLAG AND BALL

WAVE ARMS

INMARSAT

DIGITAL SELECTIVE CALLING

POSITION INDICATING RADIO BEACON

SMOKE

—INLAND—
Sound and Light Signals

Rule 37
Distress Signals

§ 83.37

When a vessel is in distress and requires assistance she shall use or exhibit the signals described in Annex IV of these Rules (33 CFR part 87) [‡].

A high intensity white light flashing at regular intervals from 50 to 70 times per minute. Inland only.

[‡] The distress signals for inland waters are the same as those displayed on the facing page for international waters, with the exception of this high intensity flashing white light.

PART E—EXEMPTIONS

Rule 38
Exemptions[‡]

Any vessel (or class of vessels) provided that she complies with the requirements of the International Regulations for Preventing Collisions at Sea, 1960, the keel of which is laid or which is at a corresponding stage of construction before the entry into force of these Regulations may be exempted from compliance therewith as follows:

(a) The installation of lights with ranges prescribed in Rule 22, until four years after the date of entry into force of these Regulations.

(b) The installation of lights with color specifications as prescribed in Section 7 of annex I to these Regulations, until four years after the date of entry into force of these Regulations.

(c) The repositioning of lights as a result of conversion from Imperial to metric units and rounding off measurement figures, permanent exemption.

(d) (i)The repositioning of masthead lights on vessels of less than 150 m in length, resulting from the prescriptions of Section 3(a) of annex I to these Regulations, permanent exemption.

[‡] Per 33 CFR 81.20, each vessel under the 72 COLREGS, except the vessels of the Navy, is exempt from the requirements of the 72 COLREGS to the limitation for the period of time stated in Rule 38 (a), (b), (c), (d), (e), (f), and (g) if: (a) Her keel was laid or is at a corresponding stage of construction before July 15, 1977; and, (b) She meets the International Regulations for Preventing Collisions at Sea, 1960 (77 Stat. 194, 33 U.S.C. 1051-1094).

—INLAND—
Exemptions

SUBPART E—EXEMPTIONS

Rule 38
Exemptions

§ 83.38

Any vessel or class of vessels, the keel of which was laid or which was at a corresponding stage of construction before December 24, 1980, provided that she complies with the requirements of—

(a) The Act of June 7, 1897 (30 Stat. 96), as amended (33 U.S.C. 154-232) for vessels navigating the waters subject to that statute;

(b) Section 4233 of the Revised Statutes (33 U.S.C. 301-356) for vessels navigating the waters subject to that statute;

(c) The Act of February 8, 1895 (28 Stat. 645), as amended (33 U.S.C. 241-295) for vessels navigating the waters subject to that statute; or

(d) Sections 3, 4, and 5 of the Act of April 25, 1940 (54 Stat. 163), as amended (46 U.S.C. 526b, c, and d) for motorboats navigating the waters subject to that statute; shall be exempted from compliance with the technical Annexes to these Rules (33 CFR parts 84 through 88) as follows:

(i) The installation of lights with ranges prescribed in Rule 22 (§ 83.22), vessels of less than 20 meters in length are permanently exempt.

(ii) The installation of lights with color specifications as prescribed in Annex I to these Rules (33 CFR part 84), vessels of less than 20 meters in length are permanently exempt;

(iii) The repositioning of lights as a result of conversion to metric units and rounding off measurement figures are permanently exempt.

(iv) The horizontal repositioning of masthead lights prescribed by Annex I to these Rules (33 CFR part 84), vessels of less than 150 meters in length are permanently exempted.

(v) Power-driven vessels of 12 meters or more but less than 20 meters in length are permanently exempt from the provisions of Rule 23(a)(i) and (iv) (§ 83.23(a)(i) and (iv)) provided that, in place of these lights, the vessel exhibits a white light aft visible all-round the horizon.

Rule 38—CONTINUED

(d) (continued)

(ii) The repositioning of masthead lights on vessels of 150 m or more in length, resulting from the prescriptions of section 3(a) of annex I to these Regulations, until nine years after the date of entry into force of these Regulations.

(e) The repositioning of masthead lights resulting from the prescriptions of section 2(b) of annex I to these Regulations, until nine years after the date of entry into force of these Regulations.

(f) The repositioning of sidelights resulting from the prescriptions of sections 2(g) and 3(b) of annex I to these Regulations, until nine years after the date of entry into force of these Regulations.

(g) The requirements for sound signal appliances prescribed in annex III to these Regulations, until nine years after the date of entry into force of these Regulations.

(h) The repositioning of all-round lights resulting from the prescription of section 9(b) of annex I to these Regulations, permanent exemption.

—INLAND—
Exemptions

[BLANK]

—INTERNATIONAL—
Annex I

Positioning and Technical Details of Lights and Shapes

1. Definition

The term *height above the hull* means height above the uppermost continuous deck. This height shall be measured from the position vertically beneath the location of the light.

2. Vertical positioning and spacing of lights

(a) On a power-driven vessel of 20 meters or more in length the masthead lights shall be placed as follows:

(i) the forward masthead light, or if only one masthead light is carried, then that light, at a height above the hull of not less than 6 meters, and, if the breadth of the vessel exceeds 6 meters, then at a height above the hull not less than such breadth, so however that the light need not be placed at a greater height above the hull than 12 meters;

(ii) when two masthead lights are carried the after one shall be at least 4.5 meters vertically higher than the forward one.

(b) The vertical separation of masthead lights of power-driven vessels shall be such that in all normal conditions of trim the after light will be seen over and separate from the forward light at a distance of 1000 meters from the stem when viewed from sea level.

(c) The masthead light of a power-driven vessel of 12 meters but less than 20 meters in length shall be placed at a height above the gunwale of not less than 2.5 meters.

(d) A power-driven vessel of less than 12 meters in length may carry the uppermost light at a height of less than 2.5 meters above the gunwale. When, however, a masthead light is carried in addition to sidelights and a sternlight or the all-round light prescribed in rule 23(d)(i) is carried in addition to sidelights, then such masthead light or all-round light shall be carried at least 1 meter higher than the sidelights.

—INLAND—
Annex I
33 CFR 84
Positioning and Technical Details of Lights and Shapes

§ 84.01 Definitions

(a) The term *height above the hull* means height above the uppermost continuous deck. This height shall be measured from the position vertically beneath the location of the light.

(b) *High-speed craft* means a craft capable of maximum speed in meters per second (m/s) equal to or exceeding: $3.7 \nabla^{0.1667}$; where ∇ = displacement corresponding to the design waterline (cubic meters).

Note to paragraph (b): The same formula expressed in pounds and knots is maximum speed in knots (kts) equal to exceeding 1.98(lbs) $3.7 \nabla^{0.1667}$; where ∇=displacement corresponding to design waterline in pounds.

(c) The term *practical cut-off* means, for vessels 20 meters or more in length, 12.5 percent of the minimum luminous intensity (Table 84.15(b)) corresponding to the greatest range of visibility for which the requirements of Annex I (33 CFR part 84) are met.

(d) The term *Rule* or *Rules* has the same meaning as in 33 CFR 83.03(r).

§ 84.02 Vertical positioning and spacing of lights

(a) On a power-driven vessel of 20 meters or more in length the masthead lights shall be placed as follows:

(i) The forward masthead light, or if only one masthead light is carried, then that light, at a height above the hull of not less than 5 meters, and, if the breadth of the vessel exceeds 5 meters, then at a height above the hull not less than such breadth, so however that the light need not be placed at a greater height above the hull than 8 meters.

(ii) When two masthead lights are carried the after one shall be at least 2 meters vertically higher than the forward one.

(b) The vertical separation of the masthead lights of power-driven vessels shall be such that in all normal conditions of trim the after light will be seen over and separate from the forward light at a distance of 1000 meters from the stem when viewed from water level.

(c) The masthead light of a power-driven vessel of 12 meters but less than 20 meters in length shall be placed at a height above the gunwale of not less than 2.5 meters.

(d) The masthead light, or the all-round light described in Rule 23(d)(§ 83.23(d) of this chapter), of a power-driven vessel of less than 12 meters in length shall be carried at least one meter higher than the sidelights.

(e) One of the two or three masthead lights prescribed for a power-driven vessel when engaged in towing or pushing another vessel shall be placed in the same position as either the forward masthead light or the after masthead light; provided that, if carried on the aftermast, the lowest after masthead light shall be at least 4.5 meters vertically higher than the forward masthead light.

(f) (i) The masthead light or lights prescribed in Rule 23(a) shall be so placed as to be above and clear of all other lights and obstructions except as described in subparagraph (ii).

(ii) When it is impracticable to carry the all-round lights prescribed by Rule 27(b)(i) or Rule 28 below the masthead lights, they may be carried above the after masthead light(s) or vertically in between the forward masthead light(s) and after masthead light(s), provided that in the latter case the requirement of Section 3(c) of this Annex shall be complied with.

(g) The sidelights of a power-driven vessel shall be placed at a height above the hull not greater than three quarters of that of the forward masthead light. They shall not be so low as to be interfered with by deck lights.

(h) The sidelights, if in a combined lantern and carried on a power-driven vessel of less than 20 meters in length, shall be placed not less than 1 meter below the masthead light.

(i) When the Rules prescribe two or three lights to be carried in a vertical line, they shall be spaced as follows:

(i) on a vessel of 20 meters in length or more such lights shall be spaced not less than 2 meters apart, and the lowest of these lights shall, except where a towing light is required, be placed at a height of not less than 4 meters above the hull;

(ii) on a vessel of less than 20 meters in length such lights shall be spaced not less than 1 meter apart and the lowest of these lights shall, except where a towing light is required, be placed at a height of not less than 2 meters above the gunwale;

(iii) when three lights are carried they shall be equally spaced.

(j) The lower of the two all-round lights prescribed for a vessel when engaged in fishing shall be at a height above the sidelights not less than twice the distance between the two vertical lights.

(k) The forward anchor light prescribed in Rule 30(a)(i), when two are carried, shall not be less than 4.5 meters above the after one. On a vessel of 50 meters or more in length this forward anchor light shall be placed at a height of not less than 6 meters above the hull.

(e) One of the two or three masthead lights prescribed for a power-driven vessel when engaged in towing or pushing another vessel shall be placed in the same position as either the forward masthead light or the after masthead light, provided that the lowest after masthead light shall be at least 2 meters vertically higher than the highest forward masthead light.

(f) (i) The masthead light or lights prescribed in Rule 23(a) (§ 83.23(a)of this chapter) shall be so placed as to be above and clear of all other lights and obstructions except as described in paragraph (f)(ii) of this section.

(ii) When it is impracticable to carry the all-round lights prescribed in Rule 27(b)(i) (§ 83.27(b)(i)of this chapter) below the masthead lights, they may be carried above the after masthead light(s) or vertically in between the forward masthead light(s) and after masthead light(s), provided that in the latter case the requirement of § 84.03(c) shall be complied with.

(g) The sidelights of a power-driven vessel shall be placed at least one meter lower than the forward masthead light. They shall not be so low as to be interfered with by deck lights.

(h) [Reserved]

(i) When the Rules in this subchapter E [‡] prescribe two or three lights to be carried in a vertical line, they shall be spaced as follows:

(i) On a vessel of 20 meters in length or more such lights shall be spaced not less than 1 meter apart, and the lowest of these lights shall, except where a towing light is required, be placed at a height of not less than 4 meters above the hull;

(ii) On a vessel of less than 20 meters in length such lights shall be spaced not less than 1 meter apart and the lowest of these lights shall, except where a towing light is required, be placed at a height of not less than 2 meters above the gunwale;

(iii) When three lights are carried they shall be equally spaced.

(j) The lower of the two all-round lights prescribed for a vessel when engaged in fishing shall be at a height above the sidelights not less than twice the distance between the two vertical lights.

(k) The forward anchor light prescribed in Rule 30(a)(i) (§ 83.30(a)(i)), when two are carried, shall not be less than 4.5 meters above the after one. On a vessel of 50 meters or more in length this forward anchor light shall be placed at a height of not less than 6 meters above the hull.

[‡] Parts 83-90 of Title 33 Code of Federal Regulations.

3. Horizontal positioning and spacing of lights

(a) When two masthead lights are prescribed for a power-driven vessel, the horizontal distance between them shall not be less than one half of the length of the vessel but need not be more than 100 meters. The forward light shall be placed not more than one quarter of the length of the vessel from the stem.

(b) On a power-driven vessel of 20 meters or more in length the sidelights shall not be placed in front of the forward masthead lights. They shall be placed at or near the side of the vessel.

(c) When the lights prescribed in Rule 27(b)(i) or Rule 28 are placed vertically between the forward masthead light(s) and the after masthead light(s) these all-round lights shall be placed at a horizontal distance of not less than 2 meters from the fore and aft centerline of the vessel in the athwartship direction.

(d) When only one masthead light is prescribed for a power-driven vessel, this light shall be exhibited forward of amidships; except that a vessel of less than 20 meters in length need not exhibit this light forward of amidships but shall exhibit it as far forward as is practicable.

4. Details of location of direction-indicating lights for fishing vessels, dredgers and vessels engaged in underwater operations

(a) The light indicating the direction of the outlying gear from a vessel engaged in fishing as prescribed in Rule 26(c)(ii) shall be placed at a horizontal distance of not less than 2 meters and not more than 6 meters away from the two all-round red and white lights. This light shall be placed not higher than the all-round white light prescribed in Rule 26(c)(i) and not lower than the sidelights.

(b) The lights and shapes on a vessel engaged in dredging or underwater operations to indicate the obstructed side and/or the side on which it is safe to pass, as prescribed in Rule 27(d)(i) and (ii), shall be placed at the maximum practical horizontal distance, but in no case less than 2 meters, from the lights or shapes prescribed in Rule 27(b)(i) and (i). In no case shall the upper of these lights or shapes be at a greater height than the lower of the three lights or shapes prescribed in Rule 27(b)(i) and (ii).

§ 84.03 Horizontal positioning and spacing of lights

(a) Except as specified in paragraph (e) of this section, when two masthead lights are prescribed for a power-driven vessel, the horizontal distance between them must not be less than one quarter of the length of the vessel but need not be more than 50 meters. The forward light must be placed not more than one half of the length of the vessel from the stem.

(b) On a power-driven vessel of 20 meters or more in length the sidelights shall not be placed in front of the forward masthead lights. They shall be placed at or near the side of the vessel.

(c) When the lights prescribed in Rule 27(b)(i) (§ 83.27(b)(i) of this chapter) are placed vertically between the forward masthead light(s) and the after masthead light(s), these all-round lights shall be placed at a horizontal distance of not less than 2 meters from the fore and aft centerline of the vessel in the athwartship direction.

(d) When only one masthead light is prescribed for a power-driven vessel, this light must be exhibited forward of amidships. For a vessel of less than 20 meters in length, the vessel shall exhibit one masthead light as far forward as is practicable.

(e) On power-driven vessels 50 meters but less than 60 meters in length operated on the Western Rivers, and those waters specified in § 89.25 of this chapter, the horizontal distance between masthead lights shall not be less than 10 meters.

§ 84.04 Details of location of direction-indicating lights for fishing vessels, dredgers and vessels engaged in underwater operations

(a) The light indicating the direction of the outlying gear from a vessel engaged in fishing as prescribed in Rule 26(c)(ii) (§ 83.26(c)(ii) of this chapter) shall be placed at a horizontal distance of not less than 2 meters and not more than 6 meters away from the two all-round red and white lights. This light shall be placed not higher than the all-round white light prescribed in Rule 26(c)(i) (§ 83.26(c)(i) of this chapter) and not lower than the sidelights.

(b) The lights and shapes on a vessel engaged in dredging or underwater operations to indicate the obstructed side and/or the side on which it is safe to pass, as prescribed in Rule 27(d)(i) and (ii) (§ 83.27(d)(i) and (ii) of this chapter), shall be placed at the maximum practical horizontal distance, but in no case less than 2 meters, from the lights or shapes prescribed in Rule 27(b)(i) and (i) (§ 83.27(b)(i) and (ii) of this chapter). In no case shall the upper of these lights or shapes be at a greater height than the lower of the three lights or shapes prescribed in Rule 27(b)(i) and (ii) (§ 83.27)(b)(i) and (ii) of this chapter).

5. Screens for sidelights

The sidelights of vessels of 20 meters or more in length shall be fitted with inboard screens painted matt black, and meeting the requirements of Section 9 of this Annex. On vessels of less than 20 meters in length the sidelights, if necessary to meet the requirements of Section 9 of this Annex, shall be fitted with inboard matt black screens. With a combined lantern, using a single vertical filament and a very narrow division between the green and red sections, external screens need not be fitted.

6. Shapes

(a) Shapes shall be black and of the following sizes:

(i) a ball shall have a diameter of not less than 0.6 meter;

(ii) a cone shall have a base diameter of not less than 0.6 meter and a height equal to its diameter;

(iii) a cylinder shall have a diameter of at least 0.6 meter and a height of twice its diameter;

(iv) a diamond shape shall consist of two cones as defined in (ii) above having a common base.

(b) The vertical distance between shapes shall be at least 1.5 meter.

(c) In a vessel of less than 20 meters in length shapes of lesser dimensions but commensurate with the size of the vessel may be used and the distance apart may be correspondingly reduced.

7. Color specification of lights

The chromaticity of all navigation lights shall conform to the following standards, which lie within the boundaries of the area of the diagram specified for each color by the International Commission on Illumination (CIE).

§ 84.05 Screens

(a) The sidelights of vessels of 20 meters or more in length shall be fitted with matt black inboard screens and meet the requirements of § 84.15. On vessels of less than 20 meters in length, the sidelights, if necessary to meet the requirements of § 84.15, shall be fitted with matt black inboard screens. With a combined lantern, using a single vertical filament and a very narrow division between the green and red sections, external screens need not be fitted.

(b) On power-driven vessels less than 12 meters in length constructed after July 31, 1983, the masthead light, or the all-round light described in Rule 23(d) (§ 83.23(d) of this chapter) shall be screened to prevent direct illumination of the vessel forward of the operator's position.

§ 84.06 Shapes

(a) Shapes shall be black and of the following sizes:

(i) A ball shall have a diameter of not less than 0.6 meter.

(ii) A cone shall have a base diameter of not less than 0.6 meters and a height equal to its diameter.

(iii) A diamond shape shall consist of two cones (as defined in paragraph (a)(ii) of this section) having a common base.

(b) The vertical distance between shapes shall be at least 1.5 meters.

(c) In a vessel of less than 20 meters in length shapes of lesser dimensions but commensurate with the size of the vessel may be used and the distance apart may be correspondingly reduced.

§ 84.13 Color specification of lights

(a) The chromaticity of all navigation lights shall conform to the following standards, which lie within the boundaries of the area of the diagram specified for each color by the International Commission on Illumination (CIE), in the "Colors of Light Signals", which is incorporated by reference. It is Publication CIE No. 2.2. (TC-1.6), 1975, and is available from the Illumination Engineering Society, 345 East 47th Street, New York, NY 10017 and is available for inspection at the Coast Guard Coast Guard Headquarters. Contact Commandant (CG–43), Attn: Office of Civil Engineering, U.S. Coast Guard Stop 7714, 2703 Martin Luther King Jr. Avenue SE., Washington, DC 20593–7714. It is also available for inspection at the National Archives and Records Administration (NARA). For information on the availability of this material at NARA, call 202–741–6030, or go to: http://www.archives.gov/federal_register/code_of_federal_regulations/ibr_locations.html. This incorporation by reference was approved by the Director of the Federal Register.

The boundaries of the area for each color are given by indicating the corner coordinates, which are as follows:

(i) White:

x 0.525	0.525	0.452	0.310	0.310	0.443
y 0.382	0.440	0.440	0.348	0.283	0.382

(ii) Green:

x 0.028	0.009	0.300	0.203
y 0.385	0.723	0.511	0.356

(iii) Red:

x 0.680	0.660	0.735	0.721
y 0.320	0.320	0.265	0.259

(iv) Yellow:

x 0.612	0.618	0.575	0.575
y 0.382	0.382	0.425	0.406

8. Intensity of lights

(a) The minimum luminous intensity of lights shall be calculated by using the formula:

$$I = 3.43 \times 10^6 \times T \times D^2 \times K^{-D}$$

where:

I is luminous intensity in candelas under service conditions,

T is threshold factor 2×10^{-7} lux,

D is range of visibility (luminous range) of the light in nautical miles,

K is atmospheric transmissivity. For prescribed lights the value of K shall be 0.8, corresponding to a meteorological visibility of approximately 13 nautical miles.

(b) A selection of figures derived from the formula is given in the following table:

Range of visibility(luminous range) of light in nautical miles	Luminous intensity of light in candelas for K = 0.8
D	I
1	0.9
2	4.3
3	12
4	27
5	52
6	94

Note: The maximum luminous intensity of navigation lights should be limited to avoid undue glare. This shall not be achieved by a variable control of the luminous intensity.

(b) The boundaries of the area for each color are given by indicating the corner co-ordinates, which are as follows:

(i) White:

| x 0.525 | 0.525 | 0.452 | 0.310 | 0.310 | 0.443 |
| y 0.382 | 0.440 | 0.440 | 0.348 | 0.283 | 0.382 |

(ii) Green:

| x 0.028 | 0.009 | 0.300 | 0.203 |
| y 0.385 | 0.723 | 0.511 | 0.356 |

(iii) Red:

| x 0.680 | 0.660 | 0.735 | 0.721 |
| y 0.320 | 0.320 | 0.265 | 0.259 |

(iv) Yellow:

| x 0.612 | 0.618 | 0.575 | 0.575 |
| y 0.382 | 0.382 | 0.425 | 0.406 |

§ 84.14 Intensity of lights

(a) The minimum luminous intensity of lights shall be calculated by using the formula:

$$I = 3.43 \times 10^6 \times T \times D^2 \times K^{-D}$$

where:

I is luminous intensity in candelas under service conditions,

T is threshold factor 2×10^{-7} lux,

D is range of visibility (luminous range) of the light in nautical miles,

K is atmospheric transmissivity. For prescribed lights the value of K shall be 0.8, corresponding to a meteorological visibility of approximately 13 nautical miles.

(b) A selection of figures derived from the formula is given in the following table (Table 84.14(b)).

Table 84.14(b)

Range of visibility (luminous range) of light in nautical miles	Minimum luminous intensity of light in candelas for K = 0.8
D	I
1	0.9
2	4.3
3	12
4	27
5	52
6	94

9. Horizontal sectors

(a)(i)In the forward direction, sidelights as fitted on the vessel shall show the minimum required intensities. The intensities shall decrease to reach practical cut-off between 1° and 3° outside the prescribed sectors.

(ii) For sternlights and masthead lights and at 22.5° abaft the beam for sidelights, the minimum required intensities shall be maintained over the arc of the horizon up to 5° within the limits of the sectors prescribed in Rule 21. From 5° within the prescribed sectors the intensity may decrease by 50% up to the prescribed limits; it shall decrease steadily to reach practical cut-off at not more than 5° outside the prescribed sectors.

(b)(i) All-round lights shall be so located as not to be obscured by masts, topmasts or structures within angular sectors of more than 6°, except anchor lights prescribed in Rule 30, which need not be placed at an impracticable height above the hull.

(ii) If it is impracticable to comply with paragraph (b)(i) of this section by exhibiting only one all-round light, two all-round lights shall be used suitably positioned or screened so that they appear, as far as practicable, as one light at a distance of one mile.

10. Vertical sectors

(a) The vertical sectors of electric lights as fitted, with the exception of lights on sailing vessels underway, shall ensure that:

(i) at least the required minimum intensity is maintained at all angles from 5° above to 5° below the horizontal;

(ii) at least 60% of the required minimum intensity is maintained from 7.5° above to 7.5° below the horizontal.

(b) In the case of sailing vessels underway the vertical sectors of electric lights as fitted shall ensure that:

(i) at least the required minimum intensity is maintained at all angles from 5° above to 5° below the horizontal;

(ii) at least 50% of the required minimum intensity is maintained from 25° above to 25° below the horizontal.

(c) In the case of lights other than electric these specifications shall be met as closely as possible.

§ 84.15 Horizontal sectors

(a) (i) In the forward direction, sidelights as fitted on the vessel shall show the minimum required intensities. The intensities shall decrease to reach practical cut-off between 1 and 3 degrees outside the prescribed sectors.

(ii) For sternlights and masthead lights and at 22.5 degrees abaft the beam for sidelights, the minimum required intensities shall be maintained over the arc of the horizon up to 5 degrees within the limits of the sectors prescribed in Rule 21 (§ 83.21 of this chapter). From 5 degrees within the prescribed sectors the intensity may decrease by 50 percent up to the prescribed limits; it shall decrease steadily to reach practical cutoff at not more than 5 degrees outside the prescribed sectors.

(b) All-round lights shall be so located as not to be obscured by masts, topmasts or structures within angular sectors of more than 6 degrees, except anchor lights prescribed in Rule 30 (§ 83.30 of this chapter), which need not be placed at an impracticable height above the hull, and the all-round white light described in Rule 23(e) (§ 83.23(e) of this chapter), which may not be obscured at all.

(c) If it is impracticable to comply with paragraph (b) of this section by exhibiting only one all-round light, two all-round lights shall be used suitably positioned or screened to appear, as far as practicable, as one light at a minimum distance of one nautical mile.

Note to paragraph (c): Two unscreened all-round lights that are 1.28 meters apart or less will appear as one light to the naked eye at a distance of one nautical mile.

§ 84.16 Vertical sectors

(a) The vertical sectors of electric lights as fitted, with the exception of lights on sailing vessels underway and on unmanned barges, shall ensure that:

(i) At least the required minimum intensity is maintained at all angles from 5 degrees above to 5 degrees below the horizontal;

(ii) At least 60 percent of the required minimum intensity is maintained from 7.5 degrees above to 7.5 degrees below the horizontal.

(b) In the case of sailing vessels underway, the vertical sectors of electric lights as fitted shall ensure that:

(i) At least the required minimum intensity is maintained at all angles from 5 degrees above to 5 degrees below the horizontal;

(ii) At least 50 percent of the required minimum intensity is maintained from 25 degrees above to 25 degrees below the horizontal.

(c) In the case of unmanned barges the minimum required intensity of electric lights as fitted shall be maintained on the horizontal.

(d) In the case of lights other than electric lights these specifications shall be met as closely as possible.

11. Intensity of non-electric lights

Non-electric lights shall so far as practicable comply with the minimum intensities, as specified in the Table given in Section 8 of this Annex.

12. Maneuvering light

Notwithstanding the provisions of paragraph 2(f) of this annex, the maneuvering light described in Rule 34(b) shall be placed in the same fore and aft vertical plane as the masthead light or lights and, where practicable, at a minimum height of 2 meters vertically above the forward masthead light, provided that it shall be carried not less than 2 meters vertically above or below the after masthead light. On a vessel where only one masthead light is carried, the maneuvering light, if fitted, shall be carried where it can best be seen, not less than 2 meters vertically apart from the masthead light.

13. High-speed Craft*

(a) The masthead light of high-speed craft may be placed at a height related to the breadth of the craft lower than that prescribed in paragraph 2(a)(i) of this annex, provided that the base angle of the isosceles triangles formed by the sidelights and masthead light, when seen in end elevation, is not less than 27°.

(b) On high-speed craft of 50 meters or more in length, the vertical separation between foremast and mainmast light of 4.5 *meters required* by paragraph 2(a)(ii) of this annex may be modified provided that such distance shall not be less than the value determined by the following formula:

$$y = \frac{(a+17\Psi)C}{1000} + 2$$

where:

y   is the height of the mainmast light above the foremast light in meters;

a   is the height of the foremast light above the water surface in service condition in meters;

Ψ   is the trim in service conditions in degrees;

C   is the horizontal separation of masthead lights in meters.

*Refer to the International Code of Safety for High-Speed Craft, 1994 and the International Code of Safety for High-Speed Craft, 2000.

14. Approval

The construction of lights and shapes and the installation of lights on board the vessel shall be to the satisfaction of the appropriate authority of the State whose flag the vessel is entitled to fly.

—INLAND—
Annex I—CONTINUED

§ 84.17 Intensity of non-electric lights
Non-electric lights shall so far as practicable comply with the minimum intensities, as specified in the Table 84.14(b).

§ 84.18 Maneuvering light
Notwithstanding the provisions of § 84.02(f), the maneuvering light described in Rule 34(b) (§ 83.34(b) of this chapter) shall be placed approximately in the same fore and aft vertical plane as the masthead light or lights and, where practicable, at a minimum height of one-half meter vertically above the forward masthead light, provided that it shall be carried not less than one-half meter vertically above or below the after masthead light. On a vessel where only one masthead light is carried the maneuvering light, if fitted, shall be carried where it can best be seen, not less than one-half meter vertically apart from the masthead light.

§ 84.19 High-speed Craft
(a) The masthead light of high-speed craft may be placed at a height related to the breadth lower than that prescribed in § 84.02(a)(i), provided that the base angle of the isosceles triangle formed by the sidelights and masthead light when seen in end elevation is not less than 27°.

(b) On high-speed craft of 50 meters or more in length, the vertical separation between foremast and mainmast light of 4.5 meters required by § 84.02(k) may be modified provided that such distance shall not be less than the value determined by the following formula:

$$y = \frac{(a + 17\Psi)C}{1000} + 2 \; ;$$

where:

    y   is the height of the mainmast light above the foremast light in meters;

    a   is the height of the foremast light above the water surface in service condition in meters;

    Ψ is the trim in service condition in degrees;

    C   is the horizontal separation of masthead lights in meters.

Note to § 84.19: Refer to the International Code of Safety for High-Speed Craft, 1994 and the International Code of Safety for High-Speed Craft, 2000

§ 84.20 Approval
The construction of lights and shapes and the installation of lights on board a vessel must satisfy the Commandant, U. S. Coast Guard.

—INTERNATIONAL—
Annex II

Additional Signals for Fishing Vessels
Fishing in Close Proximity

1. General
The lights mentioned herein shall, if exhibited in pursuance of Rule 26(d), be placed where they can best be seen. They shall be at least 0.9 meter apart but at a lower level than lights prescribed in Rule 26(b)(i) and (c)(i). The lights shall be visible all around the horizon at a distance of at least 1 mile but at a lesser distance than the lights prescribed by these Rules for fishing vessels.

2. Signals for trawlers
(a) Vessels of 20 meters or more in length when engaged in trawling, whether using demersal or pelagic gear, shall exhibit:
    (i) when shooting their nets: two white lights in a vertical line;
    (ii) when hauling their nets: one white light over one red light in a vertical line;
    (iii) when the net has come fast upon an obstruction: two red lights in a vertical line.

(b) Each vessel of 20 meters or more in length engaged in pair trawling shall exhibit:
    (i) by night, a searchlight directed forward and in the direction of the other vessel of the pair;
    (ii) when shooting or hauling their nets or when their nets have come fast upon an obstruction, the lights prescribed in 2(a) above.

(c) A vessel of less than 20 meters in length engaged in trawling, whether using demersal or pelagic gear, or engaged in pair trawling, may exhibit the lights prescribed in paragraphs (a) or (b) of this section, as appropriate.

3. Signals for purse seiners
Vessels engaged in fishing with purse seine gear may exhibit two yellow lights in a vertical line. These lights shall flash alternately every second and with equal light and occultation duration. These lights may be exhibited only when the vessel is hampered by its fishing gear.

—INLAND—
Annex II
33 CFR 85

§ 85.01. [Reserved]

—INTERNATIONAL—
Annex III

Technical Details of Sound Signal Appliances

1. Whistles
(a) Frequencies and range of audibility
The fundamental frequency of the signal shall lie within the range 70-700 Hz. The range of audibility of the signal from a whistle shall be determined by those frequencies, which may include the fundamental and/or one or more higher frequencies, which lie within the range 180-700 Hz (+/- 1%) for a vessel of 20 meters or more in length, or 180-2100 Hz (+/- 1%) for a vessel of less than 20 meters in length and which provide the sound pressure levels specified in paragraph 1(c) below.

(b) Limits of fundamental frequencies
To ensure a wide variety of whistle characteristics, the fundamental frequency of a whistle shall be between the following limits:
 (i)   70-200 Hz, for a vessel 200 meters or more in length;
 (ii) 130-350 Hz, for a vessel 75 meters but less than 200 meters in length;
 (iii) 250-700 Hz, for a vessel less than 75 meters in length.

(c) Sound signal intensity and range of audibility
A whistle fitted in a vessel shall provide, in the direction of maximum intensity of the whistle and at a distance of 1 meter from it, a sound pressure level in at least one 1/3-octave band within the range of frequencies 180-700 Hz (+/- 1%) for a vessel of 20 meters or more in length, or 180-2100 Hz (+/- 1%) for a vessel of less than 20 meters in length, of not less than the appropriate figure given in the table below.

The range of audibility in the table above is for information and is approximately the range at which a whistle may be heard on its forward axis with 90 percent probability in conditions of still air on board a vessel having average background noise level at the listening posts (taken to be 68 dB in the octave band centered on 250 Hz and 63 dB in the octave band centered on 500 Hz).

—INLAND—
Annex III
33 CFR 86
Technical Details of Sound Signal Appliances

§ 86.01 Whistles.

(a) *Frequencies and range of audibility.* The fundamental frequency of the signal shall lie within the range 70-700 Hz. The range of audibility of the signal from a whistle shall be determined by those frequencies, which may include the fundamental and/or one or more higher frequencies, which lie within the range 180-700 Hz (+/- 1%) for a vessel of 20 meters or more in length, or 180-2100 Hz (+/- 1%) for a vessel of less than 20 meters in length and which provide the sound pressure levels specified in paragraph (c) of this section.

(b) *Limits of fundamental frequencies.* To ensure a wide variety of whistle characteristics, the fundamental frequency of a whistle shall be between the following limits:
  (i)   70-200 Hz, for a vessel 200 meters or more in length.
  (ii)   130-350 Hz, for a vessel 75 meters but less than 200 meters in length.
  (iii)   250-700 Hz, for a vessel less than 75 meters in length.

(c) *Sound signal intensity and range of audibility.*
A whistle fitted in a vessel shall provide, in the direction of maximum intensity of the whistle and at a distance of 1 meter from it, a sound pressure level in at least one $1/3^{rd}$-octave band within the range of frequencies 180-700 Hz (+/- 1%) for a vessel of 20 meters *or more* in length, *or 180-2100 Hz (+/-1%) for a vessel of less than 20 meters in length,* of not less than the appropriate figure given in Table 86.01(c) of this section. The range of audibility in Table 86.01(c) is the approximate range at which a whistle may be heard on its forward axis with 90% probability in conditions of still air on board a vessel having average background noise level at the listening posts (taken to be 68 dB in the octave band centered on 250 Hz and 63 dB in the octave band centered on 500 Hz). It is shown for informational purposes only. In practice, the range at which a whistle may be heard is extremely variable and depends critically on weather conditions; the values given can be regarded as typical but under conditions of strong wind or high ambient noise level at the listening post the range may be reduced.

Length of vessel in meters	1/3-octave band level at 1 meter in dB referred to 2×10^{-5} N/m^2	Audibility range in nautical miles
200 or more	143	2
75 but less than 200	138	1.5
20 but less than 75	130	1
Less than 20	120 * 115 † 111 ‡	0.5

* When the measured frequencies lie within the range 180-450 Hz
† When the measured frequencies lie within the range 450-800 Hz
‡ When the measured frequencies lie within the range 800-2100 Hz

In practice the range at which a whistle may be heard is extremely variable and depends critically on weather conditions; the values given can be regarded as typical but under conditions of strong wind or high ambient noise level at the listening post the range may be much reduced.

(d) **Directional properties**

The sound pressure level of a directional whistle shall be not more than 4 dB below the prescribed sound pressure level on the axis at any direction in the horizontal plane within ± 45 degrees of the axis. The sound pressure level at any other direction in the horizontal plane shall be not more than 10 dB below the prescribed sound pressure level on the axis, so that the range in any direction will be at least half the range on the forward axis. The sound pressure level shall be measured in that one-third octave band which determines the audibility range.

(e) **Positioning of whistles**

When a directional whistle is to be used as the only whistle on a vessel, it shall be installed with its maximum intensity directed straight ahead.

A whistle shall be placed as high as practicable on a vessel, in order to reduce interception of the emitted sound by obstructions and also to minimize hearing damage risk to personnel. The sound pressure level of the vessel's own signal at listening posts shall not exceed 110 dB(A) and so far as practicable should not exceed 100 dB(A).

(f) **Fitting of more than one whistle**

If whistles are fitted at a distance apart of more than 100 meters, it shall be so arranged that they are not sounded simultaneously.

Table 86.01(c)

Length of vessel in meters	$\frac{1}{3}^{rd}$-octave band level at 1 meter in dB referred to $2x10^{-5}\,N/m^2$	Audibility range in nautical miles
200 or more	143	2
75 but less than 200	138	1.5
20 but less than 75	130	1
Less than 20	[1]120 [2]115 [3]111	0.5

[1] When the measured frequencies lie within the range 180-450 Hz.
[2] When the measured frequencies lie within the range 450-800 Hz.
[3] When the measured frequencies lie within the range 800-2100 Hz.

(d) *Directional properties.* The sound pressure level of a directional whistle shall be not more than 4 dB below the sound pressure level specified in paragraph (c) of this section, in any direction in the horizontal plane within ±45 degrees of the forward axis. The sound pressure level of the whistle in any other direction in the horizontal plane shall not be more than 10 dB less than the sound pressure level specified for the forward axis, so that the range of audibility in any direction will be at least half the range required on the forward axis. The sound pressure level shall be measured in that one $\frac{1}{3}^{rd}$-octave band which determines the audibility range.

(e) *Positioning of whistles*

(i) When a directional whistle is to be used as the only whistle on the vessel and is permanently installed, it shall be installed with its forward axis directed forward.

(ii) A whistle shall be placed as high as practicable on a vessel, in order to reduce interception of the emitted sound by obstructions and also to minimize hearing damage risk to personnel. The sound pressure level of the vessel's own signal at listening posts shall not exceed 110 dB(A) and so far as practicable should not exceed 100 dB(A).

(f) *Fitting of more than one whistle.* If whistles are fitted at a distance apart of more than 100 meters, they shall not be sounded simultaneously.

(g) **Combined whistle systems**

If due to the presence of obstructions the sound field of a single whistle or of one of the whistles referred to in paragraph 1(f) above is likely to have a zone of greatly reduced signal level, it is recommended that a combined whistle system be fitted so as to overcome this reduction. For the purposes of the Rules a combined whistle system is to be regarded as a single whistle. The whistles of a combined system shall be located at a distance apart of not more than 100 meters and arranged to be sounded simultaneously. The frequency of any one whistle shall differ from those of the others by at least 10 Hz.

2. **Bell or gong**

(a) **Intensity of signal**

A bell or gong, or other device having similar sound characteristics shall produce a sound pressure level of not less than 110 dB at a distance of 1 meter from it.

(b) **Construction**

Bells and gongs shall be made of corrosion-resistant material and designed to give a clear tone. The diameter of the mouth of the bell shall be not less than 300 mm for vessels of 20 meters or more in length. Where practicable, a power-driven bell striker is recommended to ensure constant force but manual operation shall be possible. The mass of the striker shall be not less than 3 percent of the mass of the bell.

3. **Approval**

The construction of sound signal appliances, their performance and their installation on board the vessel shall be to the satisfaction of the appropriate authority of the State whose flag the vessel is entitled to fly.

(g)*Combined whistle systems*
(i)   A combined whistle system is a number of whistles (sound emitting sources) operated together. For the purposes of the Rules in Subchapter E ‡ a combined whistle system is to be regarded as a single whistle.
(ii)   The whistles of a combined system shall:
(1) Be located at a distance apart of not more than 100 meters;
(2) Be sounded simultaneously;
(3) Each have a fundamental frequency different from those of the others by at least 10 Hz; and
(4) Have a tonal characteristic appropriate for the length of vessel which shall be evidenced by at least two-thirds of the whistles in the combined system having fundamental frequencies falling within the limits prescribed in paragraph (b) of this section, or if there are only two whistles in the combined system, by the higher fundamental frequency falling within the limits prescribed in paragraph (b) of this section.

Note to paragraph (g): If, due to the presence of obstructions, the sound field of a single whistle or of one of the whistles referred to in paragraph (f) of this section is likely to have a zone of greatly reduced signal level, a combined whistle system should be fitted so as to overcome this reduction.

(h)*Towing vessel whistles.* A power-driven vessel normally engaged in pushing ahead or towing alongside may, at all times, use a whistle whose characteristic falls within the limits prescribed by paragraph (b) of this section for the longest customary composite length of the vessel and its tow.

§86.02 Bell or gong

(a) *Intensity of signal.* A bell or gong, or other device having similar sound characteristics shall produce a sound pressure level of not less than 110 dB at 1 meter.

(b) *Construction.* Bells and gongs shall be made of corrosion-resistant material and designed to give clear tone. The diameter of the mouth of the bell shall be not less than 300 mm for vessels *of 20 meters or more* in length. Where practicable, a power-driven bell striker is recommended to ensure constant force but manual operation shall be possible. The mass of the striker shall be not less than 3 percent of the mass of the bell.

§ 86.03 Approval. [Reserved]

---

‡ Parts 83-90 of Title 33 Code of Federal Regulations.

—INTERNATIONAL—
Annex IV

Distress Signals

1. The following signals, used or exhibited either together or separately, indicate distress and need of assistance:

(a) a gun or other explosive signal fired at intervals of about a minute;
(b) a continuous sounding with any fog-signaling apparatus;
(c) rockets or shells, throwing red stars fired one at a time at short intervals;
(d) a signal made by any signaling method consisting of the group. . . − − − . . . (SOS) in the Morse Code;
(e) a signal sent by radiotelephony consisting of the spoken word "Mayday";
(f) the International Code Signal of distress indicated by N.C.;
(g) a signal consisting of a square flag having above or below it a ball or anything resembling a ball;
(h) flames on the vessel (as from a burning tar barrel, oil barrel, etc.);
(i) a rocket parachute flare or a hand flare showing a red light;
(j) a smoke signal giving off orange-colored smoke;
(k) slowly and repeatedly raising and lowering arms outstretched to each side;
(l) a distress alert by means of digital selective calling (DSC) transmitted on:
> (i) VHF channel 70, or
> (ii) MF/HF on the frequencies 2187.5 kHz [‡], 8414.5 kHz, 4207.5 kHz, 6312 kHz, 12577 kHz or 16804.5 kHz;

(m) a ship-to-shore distress alert transmitted by the ship's Inmarsat or other mobile satellite service provider ship earth station;
(n) signals transmitted by emergency position-indicating radio beacons;
(o) approved signals transmitted by radiocommunication systems, including survival craft radar transponders.

2. The use or exhibition of any of the foregoing signals except for the purpose of indicating distress and need of assistance and the use of other signals which may be confused with any of the above signals is prohibited.

3. Attention is drawn to the relevant sections of the International Code of Signals, the International Aeronautical and Maritime Search and Rescue Manual, Volume III, and the following signals:

(a) a piece of orange-colored canvas with either a black square and circle or other appropriate symbol (for identification from the air);
(b) a dye marker.

[‡] The U.S. Coast Guard terminated monitoring DSC safety and distress frequency 2187.5 kHz on August 1, 2013. (78 FR 42102).

—INLAND—
Annex IV
33 CFR 87
Distress Signals

§ 87.1 Need of assistance

The following signals, used or exhibited either together or separately, indicate distress and need of assistance:

(a) A gun or other explosive signal fired at intervals of about a minute;

(b) A continuous sounding with any fog-signaling apparatus;

(c) Rockets or shells, throwing red stars fired one at a time at short intervals;

(d) A signal made by any method consisting of the group . . . – – – . . . (SOS) in the Morse Code;

(e) A signal sent by radiotelephony consisting of the spoken word "Mayday";

(f) The International Code Signal of distress indicated by N.C.;

(g) A signal consisting of a square flag having above or below it a ball or anything resembling a ball;

(h) Flames on the vessel (as from a burning tar barrel, oil barrel, etc.);

(i) A rocket parachute flare or a hand flare showing a red light;

(j) A smoke signal giving off orange-colored smoke;

(k) Slowly and repeatedly raising and lowering arms outstretched to each side;

(l) A distress alert by means of digital selective calling (DSC) transmitted on:

(i) VHF channel 70, or

(ii) MF/HF on the frequencies 2187.5 kHz ‡, 8414.5 kHz, 4207.5 kHz, 6312 kHz, 12577 kHz or 16804.5 kHz;

(m) A ship-to-shore distress alert transmitted by the ship's Inmarsat or other mobile satellite service provider ship earth station;

(n) Signals transmitted by emergency position-indicating radio beacons;

(o) Signals transmitted by radiocommunication systems, including survival craft radar transponders meeting the requirements of 47 CFR 80.109; and

(p) A high intensity white light flashing at regular intervals from 50 to 70 times per minute.

§ 87.02 Exclusive use.
The use or exhibition of any of the foregoing signals except for the purpose of indicating distress and need of assistance and the use of other signals which may be confused with any of the above signals is prohibited.

§ 87.03 Supplemental signals.
Attention is drawn to the relevant sections of the International Code of Signals, the International Aeronautical and Maritime Search and Rescue Manual, Volume III, the International Telecommunication Union Radio Regulations, and the following signals:

(a) A piece of orange-colored canvas with either a black square and circle or other appropriate symbol (for identification from the air);

(b) A dye marker.

---

‡ The U.S. Coast Guard terminated monitoring DSC safety and distress frequency 2187.5 kHz on August 1, 2013. (78 FR 42102).

—INTERNATIONAL—

[BLANK]

—INLAND—
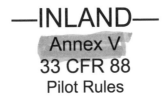
Annex V
33 CFR 88
Pilot Rules

§ 88.01 Purpose and applicability
This Part applies to all vessels operating on United States inland waters and to United States vessels operating on the Canadian waters of the Great Lakes to the extent there is no conflict with Canadian law.

§ 88.03 Definitions
The terms used in this part have the same meaning as the terms defined in Part 83 of this subchapter

.

§ 88.05 Law enforcement vessels
(a) Law enforcement vessels may display a flashing blue light when engaged in direct law enforcement or public safety activities. This light must be located so that it does not interfere with the visibility of the vessel's navigation lights.

(b) The blue light described in this section may be displayed by law enforcement vessels of the United States and the States and their political subdivisions.

§ 88.07 Public Safety Activities
(a) Vessels engaged in government sanctioned public safety activities, and commercial vessels performing similar functions, may display an alternately flashing red and yellow light signal. This identification light signal must be located so that it does not interfere with the visibility of the vessel's navigation lights. The identification light signal may be used only as an identification signal and conveys no special privilege. Vessels using the identification light signal during public safety activities must abide by the Inland Navigation Rules, and must not presume that the light or the exigency gives them precedence or right of way.

(b) Public safety activities include but are not limited to patrolling marine parades, regattas, or special water celebrations; traffic control; salvage; firefighting; medical assistance; assisting disabled vessels; and search and rescue.

—INTERNATIONAL—
INTERPRETATIVE RULES
33 CFR 82

§ 82.1 Purpose
This part contains the interpretative rules concerning the 72 COLREGS that are adopted by the Coast Guard for the guidance of the public.

§ 82.3 Pushing vessel and vessel being pushed: Composite unit
Rule 24(b) of the 72 COLREGS states that when a pushing vessel and a vessel being pushed ahead are rigidly connected in a composite unit, they are regarded as a power-driven vessel and must exhibit the lights under Rule 23. A "composite unit" is interpreted to be a pushing vessel that is rigidly connected by mechanical means to a vessel being pushed so they react to sea and swell as one vessel.

"Mechanical means" does not include the following:
(a) Lines.
(b) Hawsers.
(c) Wires.
(d) Chains.

§ 82.5 Lights for moored vessels
For the purposes of Rule 30 of the 72 COLREGS, a vessel at anchor includes a barge made fast to one or more mooring buoys or other similar device attached to the sea or river floor. Such a barge may be lighted as a vessel at anchor in accordance with Rule 30, or may be lighted on the corners in accordance with 33 CFR 83.30(h) through (l)

§ 82.7 Sidelights for unmanned barges
An unmanned barge being towed may use the exception of COLREG Rule 24(h). However, this exception only applies to the vertical sector requirements.

—INLAND—
INTERPRETATIVE RULES
33 CFR 90

§ 90.1 Purpose

This part contains the interpretative rules for the Inland Rules. These interpretative rules are intended as a guide to assist the public and promote compliance with the Inland Rules.

§ 90.3 Pushing vessel and vessel being pushed: Composite unit

Rule 24(b) of the Inland Rules states that when a pushing vessel and a vessel being pushed ahead are rigidly connected in a composite unit, they are regarded as a power-driven vessel and must exhibit the lights prescribed in Rule 23. A "composite unit" is interpreted to be the combination of a pushing vessel and a vessel being pushed ahead that are rigidly connected by mechanical means so they react to sea and swell as one vessel. Mechanical means does not include lines, wires, hawsers, or chains.

§ 90.5 Lights for moored vessels

A vessel at anchor includes a vessel made fast to one or more mooring buoys or other similar device attached to the ocean floor. Such vessels may be lighted as a vessel at anchor in accordance with Rule 30, or may be lighted on the corners in accordance with 33 CFR 83.30 (h) through (l).

§ 90.7 Sidelights for unmanned barges

An unmanned barge being towed may use the exception of COLREG Rule 24(h). However, this exception only applies to the vertical sector requirements.

—INTERNATIONAL—
PENALTY PROVISIONS
33 U.S.C. 1608

(a) Liability of vessel operator for violations

Whoever operates a vessel, subject to the provisions of this Chapter, in violation of this chapter or of any regulation promulgated pursuant to section 1607 of this title, shall be liable to a civil penalty of not more than $5,000 for each such violation.

(b) Liability of vessel for violations; seizure of vessel

Every vessel subject to the provisions of this chapter, other than a public vessel being used for noncommercial purposes, which is operated in violation of this chapter or of any regulation promulgated pursuant to section 1607 of this title, shall be liable to a civil penalty of not more than $5,000 for each such violation, for which penalty the vessel may be seized and proceeded against in the district court of the United States of any district within which such vessel may be found.

(c) Assessment of penalties; notice; opportunity for hearing; remission, mitigation, and compromise of penalty; action for collection

The Secretary of the department in which the Coast Guard is operating may assess any civil penalty authorized by this section. No such penalty may be assessed until the person charged, or the owner of the vessel charged, as appropriate, shall have been given notice of the violation involved and an opportunity for a hearing. For good cause shown, the Secretary may remit, mitigate, or compromise any penalty assessed. Upon the failure of the person charged, or the owner of the vessel charged, to pay an assessed penalty, as it may have been mitigated or compromised, the Secretary may request the Attorney General to commence an action in the appropriate district court of the United States for collection of the penalty as assessed, without regard to the amount involved, together with such other relief as may be appropriate.

—INLAND—
PENALTY PROVISIONS
33 U.S.C. 2072

(a) Liability of operator for civil penalty

Whoever operates a vessel in violation of this chapter, or of any regulation issued thereunder, or in violation of a certificate of alternative compliance issued under Rule 1 is liable to a civil penalty of not more than $5,000 for each violation.

(b) Liability of vessel for civil penalty; seizure of vessel

Every vessel subject to this chapter, other than a public vessel being used for noncommercial purposes, that is operated in violation of this chapter, or of any regulation issued thereunder, or in violation of a certificate of alternative compliance issued under Rule 1 is liable to a civil penalty of not more than $5,000 for each violation, for which penalty the vessel may be seized and proceeded against in the district court of the United States of any district within which the vessel may be found.

(c) Assessment of civil penalty by Secretary; collection

The Secretary may assess any civil penalty authorized by this section. No such penalty may be assessed until the person charged, or the owner of the vessel charged, as appropriate, shall have been given notice of the violation involved and an opportunity for a hearing. For good cause shown, the Secretary may remit, mitigate, or compromise any penalty assessed. Upon the failure of the person charged, or the owner of the vessel charged, to pay an assessed penalty, as it may have been mitigated or compromised, the Secretary may request the Attorney General to commence an action in the appropriate district court of the United States for collection of the penalty as assessed, without regard to the amount involved, together with such other relief as may be appropriate.

(d) Withholding of clearance

(1) If any owner, operator, or individual in charge of a vessel is liable for a penalty under this section, or if reasonable cause exists to believe that the owner, operator, or individual in charge may be subject to a penalty under this section, the Secretary of the Treasury, upon the request of the Secretary, shall with respect to such vessel refuse or revoke any clearance required by section 60105 of Title 46.

(2) Clearance or a permit refused or revoked under this subsection may be granted upon filing of a bond or other surety satisfactory to the Secretary.

IMPLEMENTING RULES
CERTIFICATE of ALTERNATIVE COMPLIANCE
33 CFR 81, 89

The alternative compliance procedures for the International and the Inland Rules are the same, although they appear in two distinct parts of the Code of Federal Regulations (33 CFR parts 81 and 89).

Sec.
1. Definitions.
2. General.
3. Application for a Certificate of Alternative Compliance.
4. Certificate of Alternative Compliance: Contents.
5. Certificate of Alternative Compliance: Termination.
6. Record of certification of vessels of special construction or purpose.

§ 81.1|§ 89.1 Definitions.
As used in this part:

72 COLREGS refers to the International Regulations for Preventing Collisions at Sea, 1972, done at London, October 20, 1972, as rectified by the Proces-Verbal of December 1, 1973, as amended.

Inland Rules refers to the Inland Navigation Rules contained in the Inland Navigational Rules Act of 1980 (Pub. L. 96-591) and the technical annexes established under that Act.

A vessel of special construction or purpose means a vessel designed or modified to perform a special function and whose arrangement is thereby made relatively inflexible.

Interference with the special function of the vessel occurs when installation or use of lights, shapes, or sound-signaling appliances under the 72 COLREGS/Inland Rules prevents or significantly hinders the operation in which the vessel is usually engaged.

§ 81.3|§ 89.3 General.
Vessels of special construction or purpose which cannot fully comply with the light, shape, and sound signal provisions of the 72 COLREGS/Inland Rules without interfering with their special function may instead meet alternative requirements. The Chief of the Marine Safety Division in each Coast Guard District Office makes this determination and requires that alternative compliance be as close as possible with the 72 COLREGS/Inland Rules. These regulations set out the procedure by which a vessel may be certified for alternative compliance. The information collection and recordkeeping requirements in §§ 81.5, 81.18, 89.5 and 89.19 have been approved by the Office of Management and Budget under OMB control No. 1625-0019.

§ 81.5|§ 89.5 Application for a Certificate of Alternative Compliance.

(a) The owner, builder, operator, or agent of a vessel of special construction or purpose who believes the vessel cannot fully comply with the 72 COLREGS/Inland Rules light, shape, or sound signal provisions without interference with its special function may apply for a determination that alternative compliance is justified. The application must be in writing, submitted to the Chief of the Marine Safety Division of the Coast Guard District in which the vessel is being built or operated, and include the following information:

(1) The name, address, and telephone number of the applicant.

(2) The identification of the vessel by its:

(i) Official number;

(ii) Shipyard hull number;

(iii) Hull identification number; or

(iv) State number, if the vessel does not have an official number or hull identification number.

(3) Vessel name and home port, if known.

(4) A description of the vessel's area of operation.

(5) A description of the provision for which the Certificate of Alternative Compliance is sought, including:

(i) The 72 COLREGS/Inland Rules Rule or Annex section number for which the Certificate of Alternative Compliance is sought;

(ii) A description of the special function of the vessel that would be interfered with by full compliance with the provision of that Rule or Annex section; and

(iii) A statement of how full compliance would interfere with the special function of the vessel.

(6) A description of the alternative installation that is in closest possible compliance with the applicable 72 COLREGS/Inland Rules Rule or Annex section.

(7) A copy of the vessel's plans or an accurate scale drawing that clearly shows:

(i) The required installation of the equipment under the 72 COLREGS/Inland Rules,

(ii) The proposed installation of the equipment for which certification is being sought, and

(iii) Any obstructions that may interfere with the equipment when installed in:

(A) The required location; and

(B) The proposed location.

(b) The Coast Guard may request from the applicant additional information concerning the application.

ALTERNATIVE COMPLIANCE–CONTINUED

§ 81.9|§ 89.9 Certificate of Alternative Compliance: Contents.
The Chief of the Marine Safety Division issues the Certificate of Alternative Compliance to the vessel based on a determination that it cannot comply fully with 72 COLREGS/Inland Rules light, shape, and sound signal provisions without interference with its special function. This Certificate includes:

(a) Identification of the vessel as supplied in the application under § 91.5(a)(2) or 89.5(a)(2);

(b) The provision of the 72 COLREGS/Inland Rules for which the Certificate authorizes alternative compliance;

(c) A certification that the vessel is unable to comply fully with the 72 COLREGS/Inland Rules light, shape, and sound signal requirements without interference with its special function;

(d) A statement of why full compliance would interfere with the special function of the vessel;

(e) The required alternative installation;

(f) A statement that the required alternative installation is in the closest possible compliance with the 72 COLREGS/Inland Rules without interfering with the special function of the vessel;

(g) The date of issuance;

(h) A statement that the Certificate of Alternative Compliance terminates when the vessel ceases to be usually engaged in the operation for which the certificate is issued.

§ 81.17|§ 89.17 Certificate of Alterative Compliance: Termination.
The Certificate of Alternative Compliance terminates if the information supplied under § 81.5(a)/§ 89.5(a) or the Certificate issued under § 81.9/§ 89.9 is no longer applicable to the vessel.

§ 81.18|§ 89.18 [Notice and] Record of Certification of Vessels of Special Construction or Purpose. [*Squared bracketed text COLREGS Only*]
[(a) In accordance with 33 U.S.C. 1605(c), a notice is published in the FEDERAL REGISTER if the following:

(1) Each Certificate of Alternative Compliance issued under § 81.9; and

(2) Each Coast Guard vessel determined by the Commandant to be a vessel of special construction or purpose.]

(b|a) Copies of Certificates of Alternative Compliance and documentation concerning Coast Guard vessels are available for inspection at the offices of the Marine Transportation Systems Directorate, U.S. Coast Guard Headquarters (CG–5PW), Stop 7509, 2703 Martin Luther King Jr. Avenue SE., Washington, DC 20593–7509.

(c|b) The owner or operator of a vessel issued a certificate shall ensure that the vessel does not operate unless the Certificate of Alternative Compliance or a certified copy of that certificate is on board the vessel and available for inspection by Coast Guard personnel.

144

IMPLEMENTING RULES
WATERS *UPON* WHICH CERTAIN RULES APPLY
33 CFR 89

§ 89.21 Purpose.

Inland Navigation Rules 9(a)(ii), 14(d), and 15(b) apply to the Great Lakes, and along with 24(i), apply on the "Western Rivers" as defined in Rule 3(1), and to additional specifically designated waters. The purpose of this Subpart is to specify those additional waters upon which Inland Navigation Rules 9(a)(ii), 14(d), 15(b), and 24(i) apply.

§ 89.25 Waters upon which Inland Rules 9(a)(ii), 14(d), and 15(b) apply.

Inland Rules 9(a)(ii), 14(d), and 15(b) apply on the Great Lakes, the Western Rivers, and the following specified waters:

(a) Tennessee-Tombigbee Waterway.
(b) Tombigbee River.
(c) Black Warrior River.
(d) Alabama River.
(e) Coosa River.
(f) Mobile River above the Cochrane Bridge at St. Louis Point.
(g) Flint River.
(h) Chattahoochee River.
(i) The Apalachicola River above its confluence with the Jackson River.

§ 89.27 Waters upon which Inland Rule 24(i) applies.

(a) Inland Rule 24(i) applies on the Western Rivers and the specified waters listed in § 89.25 (a) through (i).

(b) Inland Rule 24(i) applies on the Gulf Intracoastal Waterway from St. Marks, Florida, to the Rio Grande, Texas, including the Morgan City-Port Allen Alternate Route and the Galveston-Freeport Cutoff, except that a power-driven vessel pushing ahead or towing alongside shall exhibit the lights required by Inland Rule 24(c), while transiting within the following areas:

(1) St. Andrews Bay from the Hathaway Fixed Bridge at Mile 284.6 East of Harvey Locks (EHL) to the Dupont Fixed Bridge at Mile 295.4 EHL.

(2) Pensacola Bay, Santa Rosa Sound and Big Lagoon from the Light "10" off of Trout Point at Mile 176.9 EHL to the Pensacola Fixed Bridge at Mile 189.1 EHL.

(3) Mobile Bay and Bon Secour Bay from the Dauphin Island Causeway Fixed Bridge at Mile 127.7 EHL to Little Point Clear at Mile 140 EHL.

(4) Mississippi Sound from Grand Island Waterway Light "1" at Mile 53.8 EHL to Light "40" off the West Point of Dauphin Island at Mile 118.7 EHL.

(5) The Mississippi River at New Orleans, Mississippi River-Gulf Outlet Canal and the Inner Harbor Navigation Canal from the junction of the Harvey Canal and the Algiers Alternate Route at Mile 6.5 West of Harvey Locks (WHL) to the Michoud Canal at Mile 18 EHL.

(6) The Calcasieu River from the Calcasieu Lock at Mile 238.6 WHL to the Ellender Lift Bridge at Mile 243.6 WHL.

(7) The Sabine Neches Canal from Mile 262.5 WHL to Mile 291.5 WHL.

(8) Bolivar Roads from the Bolivar Assembling Basin at Mile 346 WHL to the Galveston Causeway Bridge at Mile 357.3 WHL.

(9) Freeport Harbor from Surfside Beach Fixed Bridge at Mile 393.8 WHL to the Bryan Beach Pontoon Bridge at Mile 397.6 WHL.

(10) Matagorda Ship Channel area of Matagorda Bay from Range "K" Front Light at Mile 468.7 WHL to the Port O'Connor Jetty at Mile 472.2 WHL.

(11) Corpus Christi Bay from Redfish Bay Day Beacon "55" at Mile 537.4 WHL when in the Gulf Intracoastal Waterway main route or from the north end of Lydia Ann Island Mile 531.1A when in the Gulf Intracoastal Waterway Alternate Route to Corpus Christi Bay LT 76 at Mile 543.7 WHL.

(12) Port Isabel and Brownsville Ship Channel south of the Padre Island Causeway Fixed Bridge at Mile 665.1 WHL.

COLREGS DEMARCATION LINES
33 CFR 80

GENERAL

Sec.

80.01 General basis and purpose of demarcation lines.

ATLANTIC COAST
FIRST DISTRICT

80.105 Calais, ME to Cape Small, ME.
80.110 Casco Bay, ME.
80.115 Portland Head, ME to Cape Ann, MA.
80.120 Cape Ann, MA to Marblehead Neck, MA.
80.125 Marblehead Neck, MA to Nahant, MA.
80.130 Boston Harbor entrance.
80.135 Hull, MA to Race Point, MA.
80.145 Race Point, MA to Watch Hill, RI.
80.150 Block Island, RI.
80.155 Watch Hill, RI to Montauk Point, NY.
80.160 Montauk Point, NY to Atlantic Beach, NY.
80.165 New York Harbor.
80.170 Sandy Hook, NJ to Tom's River, NJ.

FIFTH DISTRICT

80.501 Tom's River, NJ to Cape May, NJ.
80.503 Delaware Bay.
80.505 Cape Henlopen, DE to Cape Charles, VA.
80.510 Chesapeake Bay Entrance, VA.
80.515 Cape Henry, VA to Cape Hatteras, NC.
80,520 Cape Hatteras, NC to Cape Lookout, NC.
80.525 Cape Lookout, NC to Cape Fear, NC.
80.530 Cape Fear, NC to New River Inlet, NC.

SEVENTH DISTRICT

80.703 Little River Inlet, SC to Cape Romain, SC.
80.707 Cape Romain, SC to Sullivans Island, SC.
80.710 Charleston Harbor, SC.
80.712 Morris Island, SC to Hilton Head Island, SC.
80.715 Savannah River.
80.717 Tybee Island, GA to St. Simons Island, GA.
80.720 St. Simons Island, GA to Amelia Island, FL.
80.723 Amelia Island, FL to Cape Canaveral, FL.
80.727 Cape Canaveral, FL to Miami Beach, FL.
80.730 Miami Harbor, FL.
80.735 Miami, FL to Long Key, FL.

CARIBBEAN ISLANDS

80.738 Puerto Rico and Virgin Islands.

GULF COAST

SEVENTH DISTRICT

Sec.

80.740 Long Key, FL to Cape Sable, FL.
80.745 Cape Sable, FL to Cape Romano, FL.
80.748 Cape Romano, FL to Sanibel Island, FL.
80.750 Sanibel Island, FL to St. Petersburg, FL.
80.753 St. Petersburg, FL to Anclote, FL.
80.755 Anclote, FL to the Suncoast Keys, FL.
80.757 Suncoast Keys, FL to Horseshoe Point, FL.
80.760 Horseshoe Point, FL to Rock Island, FL.

EIGHTH DISTRICT

80.805 Rock Island, FL to Cape San Blas, FL.
80.810 Cape San Blas, FL to Perdido Bay, FL.
80.815 Mobile Bay, AL to the Chandeleur Island, LA.
80.825 Mississippi Passes, LA.
80.830 Mississippi Passes, LA to Point Au Fer, LA.
80.835 Point Au Fer, LA to Calcasieu Pass, LA.
80.840 Sabine Pass, TX to Galveston, TX.
80.845 Galveston, TX to Freeport, TX.
80.850 Brazos River, TX to the Rio Grande, TX.

PACIFIC COAST

ELEVENTH DISTRICT

80.1102 Santa Catalina Island, CA.
80.1104 San Diego Harbor, CA.
80.1106 Mission Bay, CA.
80.1108 Oceanside Harbor, CA.
80.1110 Dana Point Harbor, CA.
80.1112 Newport Bay, CA.
80.1114 San Pedro Bay-Anaheim Bay, CA.
80.1116 Redondo Harbor, CA.
80.1118 Marina Del Rey, CA.
80.1120 Port Hueneme, CA.
80.1122 Channel Islands Harbor, CA.
80.1124 Ventura Marina, CA.
80.1126 Santa Barbara Harbor, CA.
80.1130 San Luis Obispo Bay, CA.
80.1132 Estero-Morro Bay, CA.
80.1134 Monterey Harbor, CA.
80.1136 Moss Landing Harbor, CA.
80.1138 Santa Cruz Harbor, CA.
80.1140 Pillar Point Harbor, CA.
80.1142 San Francisco Harbor, CA.
80.1144 Bodega and Tomales Bay, CA.
80.1146 Albion River, CA.
80.1148 Noyo River, CA.
80.1150 Arcata-Humboldt Bay, CA.
80.1152 Crescent City Harbor, CA

USCG NAVIGATION RULES CORRECTIONS - ADDENDUM FOR NTM 7/18

Navigation Rules Edition 2014 - LAST NTM 50/15

Page 19—Inland Rule 9 §83.09(e)(i), line 7; read:
...sound the signal prescribed in Rule 34(d) (§83.34 (d)).
(USCG)   7/18

Page 51—Inland Rule 24 §83.24(d), line 1; read:
(d) A power-driven vessel to which paragraphs (a) or (c) of this Rule applies...
(USCG)   7/18

Page 59—Inland Rule 24 §83.24(i), line 1, change:
Designation of subparagraph (i) to (j).
(USCG)   7/18

Page 59—Inland Rule 24 §83.24(j), line 1, change:
Designation of subparagraph (j) to (i).
(USCG)   7/18

Page 59—Inland Rule 24 §83.24(i)[redesignated], line 3, read:
paragraph (a), (c) or (j) of this Rule, such vessel shall not be required to exhibit...
(USCG)   7/18

Page 99—Inland Rule 34 §83.34(a)(ii), line 4; read:
safety of the proposed maneuver, she shall sound the signal...
(USCG)   7/18

Page 149—33 CFR 80 §80.502(a), lines 3 to 5; read:
...Pullen Island across Beach Haven and Little Egg Inlet, thence across Brigantine Inlet to Brigantine Island.
(USCG)   7/18

Page 179—33 CFR 161 §161.45(b), line 2; read:
TABLE 1 to §161.45(b)—VTS ST. MARYS RIVER REPORT-ING POINTS
(USCG)   7/18

Page 179—33 CFR 166 §161.45(b), line 8; change:
Table designator 5* to 5.
(USCG)   7/18

Page 179—33 CFR 161 §161.50, line 6; read:
Tamalpais (37°55.8′ N., 122°34.6′ W.); and its navigable tributaries as far east as the port...
(USCG)   7/18

Page 180—33 CFR 161 §161.55, lines 1 to 27; replace with below:

§161.55 Vessel Traffic Service Puget Sound and the Cooperative Vessel Traffic Service for the Juan de Fuca Region. The Vessel Traffic Service for the Juan de Fuca Region. The Vessel Traffic Service for sound area consists of the

8' W.

r Point, Rhode Island, in approximate position latitude 41°27.20' N.,
sition latitude 41°23.48' N., longitude 71°02.5' W., and then to the
itude 41°24.60' N., longitude 70°57.00' W., and including all of the Cape
the confines (north of) the hurricane barrier, and the passages through

of 95°20' W.

of Exxon Dock #1 (20°43.37' N., 95°01.27' W.).

of Exxon Dock #1 (29°43.37' N., 95°01.27' W.)

dius of Point Fermin Light (33°42.3' N., 118°17.6' W.).

sland (Mile 593), only when the McAlpine upper pool gauge is at

(Saxonholm Light) at 86.0 miles Above Head of Passes (AHP), extending down river to Southwest
t Pass Entrance Light at 20.1 miles Below Head of Passes.

e drawn perpendicular on the river at 29°55'30" N and 090°12'46" W
pendicularly at 29°55.3' N 089°55.6' W (Saxonholm Light) at 86.0 miles

Port Hudson Light) at 254.5 miles AHP bounded on the south by a line
ile Point) at 109.0 miles AHP.

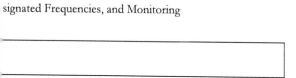

ay bounded on the east by a line drawn from Norton Point to Breezy Point; on the south
Swash Channel, and Sandy Hook Channel to Sandy Hook Point; and on the southeast
atitude 40°25' N; then west in the Raritan Bay to the Raritan River Railroad Bridge, then
Valley Draw Bridge at latitude 40°41.9' N; and then east including the waters of the Kill
est from the Holland Tunnel ventilator shaft at latitude 40°43.7' N, longitude 74°01.6' W,
of the East River to the Throgs Neck Bridge, excluding the Harlem River.

wn from Norton Point to Breezy Point; and north of a line connecting the entrance buoys
Sandy Hook Point; on the southeast including the waters of the Sandy Hook Bay south to
an Bay East Reach to a line drawn from Great Kills Light south through Raritan Bay East
ers of the Upper New York Bay south of 40°42.40' N (Brooklyn Bridge) and 40°43.70' N
Arthur Kill north of 40°38.25' N (Arthur Kill Railroad Bridge); then north into the waters
ge).

tude 40°26' N; then west of a line drawn from Great Kills Light south through the Raritan
aritan River Railroad Bridge; and north including the waters of the Arthur Kill to 40°28.25'
River north of 40°42.40' N (Brooklyn Bridge) to the Throgs Neck Bridge, excluding the

70' N.; Port Arthur Canal; Sabine Pass Channel; Sabine Bank Channel; Sabine Outer Bar
to its intersection with the Sabine-Neches Canal.
ne-Neches Waterway north of 29°52.70' N.; and the ICW from its intersection with the

annel; and the ICW from MM 260 to MM 191.

of 60° N., and west of 146°30' W.; and, all navigable waters in Port Valdez.

a of a line connecting Nodule Point and Bush Point in Admiralty Inlet and south of a line
Whidbey Island to the shoreline.
ncluding waters south and east of a line drawn from Church Point on Vancouver Island, to
border at 48°17.88' N. / 123°14.1' W., north-easterly to Hein Bank in position 48°21.094'
and, along the shoreline to Lime Kiln Light, to Kellett Bluff Light on Henry Island, along
int of Henry Island, to the southernmost point on Stuart Island in position 48°39.46' N. /
oint on Waldron Island, along the shoreline to Point Hammond, to Patos Island Light, to
rth to Boundary Bay in position 49°00.125' N. / 122°52.228' W., then due east along the
ecting Nodule Point and Bush Point and all waters east of Whidbey Island north of a line
hidbey Island to the shoreline.

of Vancouver Island including the waters north of 48° N., and east of 125°15.00' W.

, Boundary Pass, and Haro Strait north and west a line drawn from Church Point on
tion of the U.S./Canadian border at 48°17.883' N. / 123°14.1' W., north-easterly to Hein
e Point Light on San Juan Island, along the shoreline to Lime Kiln Light, to Kellett Bluff
n Point at the northernmost point of Henry Island, to the southernmost point on Stuart
ine to Turn Point Light, to Sandy Point on Waldron Island, along the shoreline to Point
389' N. / 122°52.227' W., then due north to Boundary Bay in position 49°00.125' N. /
e shoreline in Semiahmoo Bay.

Area, the navigable waters shoreward of the San Francisco Offshore Precautionary Area
rough the Golden Gate, and the navigable waters of San Francisco Bay and as far east as
ort of Sacramento on the Sacramento River.
amalpais (37°55.8' N., 122°34.6' W.) west of 122°42.0' W. and south of 37°40.0' N and

f Light) and 46°38.7' N. (Ile Parisienne Light), except the St. Marys Falls Canal and those
a Pointe to Sims Point in Potagannissing Bay and Worsley Bay).

[4] Some monitoring areas extend beyond navigable waters. Although not required, users are strongly encouraged to maintain a listening watch on the designated monitoring frequency in these areas. Otherwise, they are required to maintain watch as stated in 47 CFR 80.148.

[5] In addition to the vessels denoted in §161.16 of this chapter, requirements set forth in subpart B of this part also apply to any vessel transiting VMRS Buzzards Bay required to carry a bridge-to-bridge radiotelephone by part 26 of this chapter.

[6] Until otherwise directed, full VTS services will not be available in the Calcasieu Channel, Calcasieu River Channel, and the ICW from MM 260 to MM 191. Vessels may contact Port Arthur Traffic on the designated VTS frequency to request advisories, but are not required to monitor the VTS frequency in this sector.

[7] A Cooperative Vessel Traffic Service was established by the United States and Canada within adjoining waters. The appropriate Center administers the rules issued by both nations; however, enforces only its own set of rules within its jurisdiction. Note, the bridge-to-bridge navigational frequency, 156.650 MHz (Ch. 13), is not so designated in Canadian waters, therefore users are encouraged and permitted to make passing arrangements on the designated monitoring frequencies.

Table 1 to § 161.12(c) – VTS and VMRS Centers, Call Signs/MMSI,

Center –MMSI[1] *Call Sign*	Designated frequency (Channel Designation) –purpose[2]	Monitoring area [3,4]
San Francisco		
—003669956		
San Francisco Traffic	156.700 MHz (Ch. 14)	The navigable waters of the San Francisco Offshore Precautio east of 122°42.0' W. and north of 37°40.0' N. extending eastw
San Francisco Traffic	156.600 MHz (Ch. 12)	the port of Stockton on the San Joaquin River, as far north as The navigable waters within a 38 nautical mile radius of Mor excluding the San Francisco Offshore Precautionary Area.
St. Marys River		
—003669953		
Soo Traffic	156.600 MHz (Ch. 12)	The waters of the St. Marys River between 45°57' N. (De Tou navigable waters east of a line from 46°04.16' N. and 46°01.57

NOTES:

[1] Maritime Mobile Service Identifier (MMSI) is a unique nine-digit number assigned that identifies ship stations, ship earth stations, coast stations, coast earth stations, and group calls for use by a digital selective calling (DSC) radio, an INMARSAT ship earth station or AIS. AIS requirements are set forth in §161.21. The requirements set forth in §§161.21 and 164.46 of this subchapter apply in those areas denoted with a MMSI number, except for Louisville and Los Angeles/Long Beach.

[2] In the event of a communication failure, difficulties or other safety factors, the Center may direct or permit a user to monitor and report on any other designated monitoring frequency or the bridge-to-bridge navigational frequency, 156.650 MHz (Channel 13) or 156.375 MHz (Ch. 67), to the extent that doing so provides a level of safety beyond that provided by other means. The bridge-to-bridge navigational frequency, 156.650 MHz (Ch. 13), is used in certain monitoring areas where the level of reporting does not warrant a designated frequency.

[3] All geographic coordinates (latitude and longitude) are expressed in North American Datum of 1983 (NAD 83).

Table 1 to § 161.12(c) – VTS and VMRS Centers, Call Signs/MMSI

Center –MMSI[1] *Call Sign*	Designated frequency (Channel Designation) –purpose[2]	Monitoring area [3, 4]
New York		
—003669951		
New York Traffic	156.550 MHz (Ch. 11) —For Sailing Plans only 156.600 MHz (Ch. 12) —For vessels at anchor	The area consists of the navigable waters of the Lower New Y by a line connecting the entrance buoys at the Ambrose Ch including the waters of Sandy Hook Bay south to a line draw north into waters of the Arthur Kill and Newark Bay to the I Van Kull and the Upper New York Bay north to a line drawn in the Hudson River; and then continuing east including the w
New York Traffic	156.700 MHz (Ch. 14)	The navigable waters of the Lower New York Bay west of a li of Ambrose Channel, Swash Channel, and Sandy Hook Chann a line drawn at latitude 40°25' N; then west into the waters of Reach LGB #14 to Comfort PT, NJ; then north including the (Holland Tunnel Ventilator Shaft); west through the KVK int of the Newark Bay, south of 40°41.95' N (Lehigh Valley Draw
New York Traffic	156.600 MHz (Ch. 12)	The navigable waters of the Raritan Bay south to a line drawn Bay East Reach LGB #14 to Point Comfort, NJ; then west to N (Arthur Kill Railroad Bridge); including the waters of the Harlem River.
Port Arthur		
—003669955		
Port Arthur Traffic	156.050 MHz (Ch. 01A)	The navigable waters of the Sabine-Neches Canal south of 2 Channel; the offshore safety fairway; and the ICW from High
Port Arthur Traffic	156.275 MHz (Ch 65A)	The navigable waters of the Neches River; Sabine River; and Sabine River to MM 260.
Port Arthur Traffic	156.675 MHz (Ch 73)6	The navigable waters of the Calcasieu Channel; Calcasieu Rive
Prince William Sound		
—003669958		
Valdez Traffic	156.650 MHz (Ch. 13)	The navigable waters south of 61°05' N., east of 147°20' W., r
Puget Sound [7]		
Seattle Traffic	156.700 MHz (Ch. 14)	The waters of Puget Sound, Hood Canal and adjacent waters
—003669957		drawn due east from the southernmost tip of Possession Poin
	156.250 MHz (Ch. 5A)	The U.S. waters of the Strait of Juan de Fuca east of 124°40.00' Race Rocks Light, due east to the intersection of the U.S./Can N. / 123°02.672' W., northerly to Cattle Point Light on San Ju the shoreline to the tip of McCracken Point at the northernmo 123°11.08' W., along the shoreline to Turn Point Light, to San Alden Bank in position 48°50.39' N. / 122°52.227' W., then d international boundary to the shoreline in Semiahmoo Bay line drawn due east from the southernmost tip of Possession Point
Prince Rupert Traffic —003160013	156.725 MHz (Ch. 74)	The waters west of 124°40' W. within 12 nautical miles of the c
Victoria Traffic —03160010	156.550 MHz (Ch. 11)	The waters of the Strait of Georgia, including Vancouver H Vancouver Island, to Race Rocks Light, due easterly to the int Bank in position 48°21.093' N. / 123°02.762' W., northerly to Light on Henry Island, along the shoreline to the tip of McC Island in position 48°39.467' N. / 123°11.083' W., along the s Hammond, to Patos Island Light, to Alden Bank in position 122°52.227' W., then due east along the international boundary

Center —MMSI[1] Call Sign	Designated frequency (Channel Designation) —purpose[2]	Monitoring area [3, 4]
Berwick Bay —03669950 *Berwick Traffic*	156.550 MHz (Ch. 11)	The waters south of 29°45' N., west of 91°10' W., north of 29°37' N., and east
Buzzards Bay *Buzzards Bay Control*[5]	156.550 MHz (Ch. 11)	The waters east and north of a line drawn from the southern tangent of S longitude 71°11.70' W., to the Buzzards Bay Entrance Light in approxim southwestern tangent of Cuttyhunk Island, Massachusetts, at approximate posi Cod Canal to its eastern entrance, except that the area of New Bedford harbor the Elizabeth Islands, is not considered to be "Buzzards Bay".
Houston-Galveston —003669954		The navigable waters north of 29° N., west of 94°20' W., south of 29°49' N., a
Houston Traffic	156.550 MHz (Ch. 11) 156.250 MHz (Ch. 5A) —For Sailing Plans only	The navigable waters north of a line extending due west from the southern mo
Houston Traffic	156.600 MHz (Ch. 12) 156.250 MHz (Ch. 5A) —For Sailing Plans only	The navigable waters south of a line extending due west from the southern mo
Los Angeles/Long Beach *San Pedro Traffic*	156.700 MHz (Ch.14)	*Vessel Movement Reporting System Area:* The navigable waters within a 25 nautical
Louisville *Louisville Traffic*	156.650 MHz (Ch. 13)	The waters of the Ohio River between McAlpine Locks (Mile 606) and Twelve approximately 13.0 feet or above.
Lower Mississippi River[6] —0036699952 *New Orleans Traffic*	156.700 MHz (Ch.11)	The navigable waters of the Lower Mississippi River below 29°55.3' N 089°5 Pass, and, within a 12 nautical mile radius around 28°54.3' N 089°25.7' W (Sc
New Orleans Traffic	156.600 MHz (Ch.12)	The navigable waters of the Lower Mississippi River bounded on the north (Upper Twelve Mile Point) at 109.0 miles AHP and on the south by a line dra AHP.
New Orleans Traffic	156.600 MHz (Ch.05A)	The navigable waters of the Lower Mississippi River below 30°38.7' N 091°17 drawn perpendicular on the river at 29°55'30" N and 090°12'46" W (Upper Tw

Page 99—Inland Rule 34 §83.34(c)(ii), line 2; read:
sound a similar sound signal. If in doubt, she shall sound the signal...
(USCG) 7/18

Page 123—Inland Annex I §84.15(b), lines 1 to 12; replace with below:

(b)(i) All-round lights shall be so located as not to be obscured by masts, topmasts or structures within angular sectors of more than 6 degrees, except anchor lights prescribed in Rule 30 (§ 83.30 of this chapter), which need not be placed at an impracticable height above the hull, and the all-round white light described in Rule 23(e) (§ 83.23(e) of this chapter), which may not be obscured at all.

(b)(ii) If it is impracticable to comply with paragraph (b)(i) of this section by exhibiting only one all-round light, two all-round lights shall be used suitably positioned or screened to appear, as far as practicable, as one light at a minimum distance of one nautical mile.

Note to paragraph (b)(ii): Two unscreened all-round lights that are 1.28 meters apart or less will appear as one light to the naked eye at a distance of one nautical mile.
(USCG) 7/18

Page 148—33 CFR 80 §80.155(b), line 3; read:
Light); thence to 41°12'22.900" N., 072°06'24.700" ...
(USCG) 7/18

from the Washington State coastline at 48°23.133' N., 124°43.616' W. on Cape Flattery to the Cape Flattery Light at 48°23.5' N., 124°44.2' W. on Tatoosh Island, due west to the U.S. Territorial Sea Boundary; thence northward along the U.S. Territorial Sea Boundary to its intersection with the U.S./Canada International Boundary; thence east along the U.S./Canada International Boundary to 49°00.1' N., 122°45.3' W. (International Boundary Range C Rear Light).

(a) Vessel Traffic Service Puget Sound participates in a U.S./Canadian Cooperative Vessel Traffic Service (CVTS) to jointly manage vessel traffic in the Juan de Fuca Region. The CVTS for the Juan de Fuca Region consists of all navigable waters of the Salish Sea, bounded on the northwest by 48°35.749' N.; and on the southwest by 48°23.5' N.; and on the west by the rhumb line joining 48°35.749' N., 124°47.5' W. with 48°23.5' N., 124°48.616' W.; and on the northeast by a line drawn along 49° N. from Vancouver Island to Semiahmoo Bay; and on the southeast, by a line drawn from McCurdy Point on the Quimper Peninsula to Point Partridge on Whidbey Island. Canadian and United States Vessel Traffic Centers (Prince Rupert, B.C., Canada, Vancouver, BC, Canada and Seattle, WA) manage traffic within the CVTS area irrespective of the International Boundary.
(USCG) 7/18

Page 187 to Page 189; Table 161.12(c):
Replace with table from back of this Subsection.
(USCG) 7/18

GENERAL

§ 80.01 General basis and purpose of demarcation lines.

(a) The regulations in this part establish the lines of demarcation delineating those waters upon which mariners shall comply with the International Regulations for Preventing Collisions at Sea, 1972 (72 COLREGS) and those waters upon which mariners shall comply with the Inland Navigation Rules.

(b) The waters inside of the lines are Inland Rules Waters. The waters outside the lines are COLREGS Waters.

ATLANTIC COAST

FIRST DISTRICT

§ 80.105 Calais, ME to Cape Small, ME.

The 72 COLREGS shall apply on the harbors, bays, and inlets on the east coast of Maine from International Bridge at Calais, ME to the southwesternmost extremity of Bald Head at Cape Small.

§ 80.110 Casco Bay, ME.

(a) A line drawn from the southwesternmost extremity of Bald Head at Cape Small to the southeasternmost extremity of Ragged Island; thence to the southern tangent of Jaquish Island thence to Little Mark Island Monument Light; thence to the northernmost extremity of Jewell Island.

(b) A line drawn from the tower on Jewell Island charted in approximate position latitude 43°40.6' N., longitude 70°05.9' W. to the northeasternmost extremity of Outer Green Island.

(c) A line drawn from the southwesternmost extremity of Outer Green Island to Ram Island Ledge Light; thence to Portland Head Light.

§ 80.115 Portland Head, ME to Cape Ann, MA.

(a) Except inside lines specifically described in this section, the 72 COLREGS shall apply on the harbors, bays, and inlets on the east coast of Maine, New Hampshire, and Massachusetts from Portland Head to Halibut Point at Cape Ann.

(b) A line drawn from the southernmost tower on Gerrish Island charted in approximate position latitude 43°04.0' N., longitude 70°41.2' W. to Whaleback Light; thence to Jeffrey Point Light 2A; thence to the northeasternmost extremity of Frost Point.

(c) A line drawn from the northernmost extremity of Farm Point to Annisquam Harbor Light.

§ 80.120 Cape Ann, MA to Marblehead Neck, MA.

(a) Except inside lines specifically described in this section, the 72 COLREGS shall apply on the harbors, bays and inlets on the east coast of Massachusetts from Halibut Point at Cape Ann to Marblehead Neck.

(b) A line drawn from Gloucester Breakwater Light to the twin towers charted in approximate position latitude 42°35.1' N., longitude 70°41.6' W.

(c) A line drawn from the westernmost extremity of Gales Point to the easternmost extremity of House Island; thence to Bakers Island Light; thence to Marblehead Light.

§ 80.125 Marblehead Neck, MA to Nahant, MA.

The 72 COLREGS apply on the harbors, bays, and inlets on the east coast of Massachusetts from Marblehead Neck to the easternmost tower at Nahant, charted in approximate position latitude 42°25.4' N., longitude 70°54.6' W.

§ 80.130 Boston Harbor entrance.

A line drawn from the easternmost tower at Nahant, charted in approximate position latitude 42°25.4' N., longitude 70°54.6' W., to Boston Lighted Horn Buoy "B"; thence to the easternmost radio tower at Hull, charted in approximate position latitude 42°16.7' N., longitude 70°52.6' W.

§ 80.135 Hull, MA to Race Point, MA.

(a) Except inside lines described in this section, the 72 COLREGS apply on the harbors, bays, and inlets on the east coast of Massachusetts from the easternmost radio tower at Hull, charted in approximate position latitude 42°16.7' N., longitude 70°52.6' W., to Race Point on Cape Cod.

(b) A line drawn from Canal Breakwater Light 4 south to the shoreline.

§ 80.145 Race Point, MA to Watch Hill, RI.

(a) Except inside lines specifically described in this section, the 72 COLREGS shall apply on the sounds, bays, harbors and inlets along the coast of Cape Cod and the southern coasts of Massachusetts and Rhode Island from Race Point to Watch Hill.

(b) A line drawn from Nobska Point Light to Tarpaulin Cove Light on the southeastern side of Naushon Island; thence from the southernmost tangent of Naushon Island to the easternmost extremity of Nashawena Island; thence from the southwestern most extremity of Nashawena Island to the easternmost extremity of Cuttyhunk Island; thence from the southwestern tangent of Cuttyhunk Island to the tower on Gooseberry Neck charted in approximate position latitude 41°29.1' N., longitude 71°02.3' W.

(c) A line drawn from Sakonnet Breakwater Light 2 tangent to the southernmost part of Sachuest Point charted in approximate position latitude 41° 28.5' N., longitude 71°14.8' W.

(d) An east-west line drawn through Beavertail Light between Brenton Point and the Boston Neck shoreline.

§ 80.150 Block Island, RI.

The 72 COLREGS shall apply on the harbors of Block Island.

§ 80.155 Watch Hill, RI to Montauk Point, NY.

(a) *A line drawn from 41°18'13.999" N., 071° 51'30.300" W. (Watch Hill Light) to East Point on Fishers Island.*

(b) *A line drawn from Race Point at 41°14'36.509" N., 072°02'49.676" W. (Race Rock Light); thence to 41° 12'22.900" N., 072°06'24.700" W. (Little Gull Island Light) thence to East Point on Plum Island.*

(c) *A line drawn from 41°10'16.704" N., 072° 12'21.684' W. (Plum Island Harbor East Dolphin Light) to 41°10'17.262" N., 072°12'23.796" W. (Plum Island Harbor West Dolphin Light).*

(d) *A line drawn from 41°10'25.745" N., 072° 12'42.137" W. (Plum Island Light) to 41°09'48.393" N., 072°13'25.014" W. (Orient Point Light); thence to Orient Point.*

(e) *A line drawn from the 41°06'35.100" N.,072° 16'48.000" W. (Long Beach Bar Light) to Cornelius Point.*

(f) *A line drawn from 41°04'12.000" N., 072° 16'48.000" W (Coecles Harbor Entrance Light) to Sungic Point.*

(g) *A line drawn from Nicholl Point to 41°02'25.166", 072° 15'42.971" W. (Cedar Island Light 3CI).*

(h) *A line drawn from 41°02'06.060" N., 072° 11'19.560" W. (Threemile Harbor West Breakwater Light) to 41°02'05.580" N., 072°11'15.777" W. (Threemile Harbor East Breakwater Light).*

(i) *A line drawn from 41°04'44.210" N., 071° 56'20.308" W. (Montauk West Jetty Light 2) to 41° 04'46.095" N., 071°56'14.168" W. (Montauk East Jetty Light 1).*

§ 80.160 Montauk Point, NY to Atlantic Beach, NY.

(a) *A line drawn from 40°50'17.952" N., 072°28'29.010" W. (Shinnecock Inlet Breakwater Light 2) to 40°50'23.490" N., 072°28'40.122" W. (Shinnecock Inlet Breakwater Light 1).*

(b) *A line drawn from 40°45'47.763" N., 072°45'11.095" W. (Moriches Inlet Breakwater Light 2) to 40°45'49.692" N., 072°45'21.719" W. (Moriches Inlet Breakwater Light 1).*

(c) *A line drawn from the westernmost point on Fire Island to the southernmost extremity of the spit of land at the western end of Oak Beach.*

(d) *A line drawn from 40°34'23.568" N., 073°34'32.364" (Jones Inlet Light) 322° true across Jones Inlet to the shoreline.*

§ 80.165 New York Harbor.

A line drawn from 40°34'23.568" N., 073° 34'32.364" W. (East Rockaway Inlet Breakwater Light) to 40°27'42.177" N., 074°00'07.309" W. (Sandy Hook Light).

§ *80.501 Sandy Hook, NJ to Toms River, NJ.*

(a) *A line drawn across the seaward extremity of Shark River Inlet.*

(b) *A line drawn across the seaward extremity of Manasquan Inlet.*

(c) *A line drawn across the seaward extremity of Barnegat Inlet.*

§ *80.502 Toms River, NJ to Cape May, NJ.*

(a) *A line drawn from the seawardtangent of Long Beach Island to the seaward tangent to Pullen Island across Beach Haven and Little Egg Inlets, thence across Brigantine Inlet to Brigantine Island.*

(b) *A line drawn from the seaward extremity of Absecon Inlet.*

(c) *A line drawn parallel with the general trend of highwater shoreline from the southernmost point of Longport at latitude 39°17.6' N., longitude 74°33.1'*
        W. across Great Egg Harbor Inlet.

(d) *A line drawn parallel with the general trend of highwater shoreline across Corson Inlet.*

(e) *A line formed by the centerline of the Townsend Inlet Highway Bridge.*

(f) *A line formed by the shoreline of Seven Mile Beach to 39°00'23.757" N., 074°47'28.017" W. (Hereford Inlet Light).*

(g) *A line drawn across the seaward extremity of Cape May Inlet.*

§ **80.503 Delaware Bay.**

A line drawn from Cape May Light to Harbor

of Refuge Light; thence to the northernmost extremity of Cape Henlopen.

§ **80.505 Cape Henlopen, DE to Cape Charles, VA.**

(a) A line drawn from the seaward extremity of Indian River Inlet North Jetty to Indian River Inlet South Jetty Light.

(b) A line drawn from Ocean City Inlet Light 6 225° true across Ocean City Inlet to the submerged south breakwater.

(c) A line drawn from Assateague Beach Tower Light to the tower charted at latitude 37°52.6' N., longitude 75°26.7' W.

(d) A line formed by the range of Wachapreague Inlet Light 3 and Parramore Beach Lookout Tower drawn across Wachapreague Inlet.

(e) A line drawn from the lookout tower charted on the northern end of Hog Island to the seaward tangent of Parramore Beach.

(f) A Line drawn 207° true from the lookout tower charted on the southern end of Hog Island across Great Machipongo Inlet.

(g) A line formed by the range of the two cupolas charted on the southern end of Cobb Island drawn across Sand Shoal Inlet.

(h) Except as provided elsewhere in this section from Cape Henlopen to Cape Charles, lines drawn parallel with the general trend of the highwater shoreline across the entrances to small bays and inlets.

§ **80.510 Chesapeake Bay Entrance, VA.**

A line drawn from Cape Charles Light to Cape Henry Light.

§ **80.515 Cape Henry, VA to Cape Hatteras, NC.**

(a) A line drawn from Rudee Inlet Jetty Light 2 to Rudee Inlet Jetty Light 1.

(b) A line formed by the centerline of the highway bridge across Oregon Inlet.

§ **80.520 Cape Hatteras, NC to Cape Lookout, NC.**

§ (a) A line drawn from Hatteras Inlet Lookout Tower at latitude 35°11.8' N., longitude 75°43.9' W. 255° true to the eastern end of Ocracoke Island.

(b) A line drawn from the westernmost extremity of Ocracoke Island at latitude 35°04.0' N., longitude 76°00.8' W., to the northeastern most extremity of Portsmouth Island at latitude 35°03.7' N., longitude 76°02.3' W.

§ (c) A line drawn across Drum Inlet parallel with the general trend of the highwater shoreline.

§ **80.525 Cape Lookout, NC to Cape Fear, NC.**

(a) A line drawn from Cape Lookout Light to the seaward tangent of the southeastern end of Shackleford Banks.

(b) A line drawn from Morehead City Channel Range Front Light to the seaward extremity of the Beaufort Inlet west jetty.

(c) A line drawn from the southernmost extremity of Bogue Banks at latitude 34°38.7' N., longitude 77°06.0' W., across Bogue Inlet to the northernmost extremity of Bear Beach at latitude 34° 38.5' N., longitude 77°07.1' W.

(d) A line drawn from the easternmost extremity on the southern side of New River Inlet at latitude 34°31.5' N., longitude 77°20.6' W., to the shoreline on the northeast side on New River Inlet.

(e) A line drawn across New Topsail Inlet between the closest extremities of the shore on either side of the inlet parallel with the general trend of the highwater shoreline.

(f) A line drawn from the seaward extremity of the jetty on the northeast side of Masonboro Inlet to the seaward extremity of the jetty on the southeast side of the Inlet.

(g) Except as provided elsewhere in this section from Cape Lookout to Cape Fear, lines drawn parallel with the general trend of the highwater shoreline across the entrance of small bays and inlets.

§ 80.530 Cape Fear, NC to Little River Inlet, NC.

(a) A line drawn from the abandoned lighthouse charted in approximate position latitude 33° 52.4' N., longitude 78°00.1' W., across the Cape Fear River Entrance to Oak Island Light.

(b) Except as provided elsewhere in this section from Cape Fear to Little River Inlet, lines drawn parallel with the general trend of the highwater shoreline across the entrance to small inlets.

SEVENTH DISTRICT

§ 80.703 Little River Inlet, SC to Cape Romain, SC.

(a) A line drawn from the westernmost extremity of the sand spit on Bird Island to the easternmost extremity of Waties Island across Little River Inlet.

(b) From Little River Inlet, a line drawn parallel with the general trend of the highwater shoreline across Hog Inlet; thence a line drawn from Murrels Inlet Light 2 to Murrels Inlet Light 1; thence a line drawn parallel with the general trend of the highwater shoreline across Midway Inlet, Pawleys Inlet and North Inlet.

(c) A line drawn from the charted position of Winyah Bay North Jetty End Buoy 2N south to the Winyah Bay South Jetty.

(d) A line drawn from Santee Point to the seaward tangent of Cedar Island.

(e) A line drawn from Cedar Island Point west to Murphy Island.

(f) A north-south line from the northernmost extremity of Cape Island Point to Murphy Island.

§ 80.707 Cape Romain, SC to Sullivans Island, SC.

(a) A line drawn from the westernmost extremity of Cape Romain to the southeasternmost point on Raccoon Key.

(b) A line drawn from the westernmost extremity of Raccoon Key to the northernmost extremity of Northeast Point.

(c) A line drawn from the southernmost extremity of Bull Island to the easternmost extremity of Capers Island.

(d) A line formed by the overhead power cable from Capers Island to Dewees Island. A line formed by the overhead power cable from Dewees Island to Isle of Palms.

(e) A line formed by the centerline of the highway bridge between Isle of Palms and Sullivans Island over Breach Inlet.

§ 80.710 Charleston Harbor, SC.

(a) A line formed by the submerged north jetty from the shore to the west end of the north jetty.

(b) A line drawn from across the seaward extremity of the Charleston Harbor Jetties.

(c) A line drawn from the west end of the South Jetty across the South Entrance to Charleston Harbor to shore on a line formed by the submerged south jetty.

§ 80.712 Morris Island, SC to Hilton Head Island, SC.

(a) A line drawn from the easternmost tip of Folly Island to 32°41'37" N., 079°53'03" W. (abandoned lighthouse tower) on the northside of Lighthouse Inlet; thence west to the shoreline of Morris Island.

(b) A straight line drawn from the seaward tangent of Folly Island across Stono River to the shoreline of Sandy Point.

(c) A line drawn from the southernmost extremity of Seabrook Island 257° true across the North Edisto River Entrance to the shore of Botany Bay Island.

(d) A line drawn from the microwave antenna tower on Edisto Beach charted in approximate position latitude 32°29.3' N., longitude 80°19.2' W., across St. Helena Sound to the abandoned lighthouse tower on Hunting Island.

(e) A line formed by the centerline of the highway bridge between Hunting Island and Fripp Island.

(f) A line drawn from the westernmost extremity of Bull Point on Capers Island to Port Royal Sound Channel Range Rear Light, latitude 32°13.7' N., longitude 80°36.0' W.; thence 259° true to the easternmost extremity of Hilton Head at latitude 32°13.7' N., longitude 80°40.1' W.

§ 80.715 Savannah River.

A line drawn from the southernmost tank on Hilton Head Island charted in approximate position latitude 32°06.7' N., longitude 80°49.3' W., to Bloody Point Range Rear Light; thence to Tybee Light.

§ 80.717 Tybee Island, GA to St. Simons Island, GA.

(a) A line drawn from the southernmost extremity of Savannah Beach on Tybee Island 255° true across Tybee Inlet to the shore of Little Tybee Island south of the entrance to Buck Hammock Creek.

(b) A straight line drawn from the northeasternmost extremity of Wassaw Island 031° true through Tybee River Daybeacon 1 to the shore of Little Tybee Island. A line drawn approximately parallel with the general trend of the highwater shorelines from the seaward tangent of Wassaw Island to the seaward tangent of Bradley Point on Ossabaw Island.

(c) A north-south line (longitude 81°08.4' W.) drawn from the southernmost extremity of Ossabaw Island to St. Catherines Island.

(d) A north-south line (longitude 81°10.6' W.) drawn from the southernmost extremity of St. Catherines Island to North-east Point on Blackbeard Island.

(e) A line following the general trend of the seaward highwater shoreline across Cabretta Inlet.

(f) A north-south line (longitude 81°16.9' W.) drawn from the southwesternmost point on Sapelo Island to Wolf Island.

(g) A north-south line (longitude 81°17.1' W.) drawn from the southeasternmost point of Wolf Island to the northeasternmost point on Little St. Simons Island.

(h) A line drawn from the northeasternmost extremity of Sea Island 045° true to Little St. Simons Island.

(i) An east-west line from the southernmost extremity of Sea Island across Goulds Inlet to St. Simons Island.

§ 80.720 St. Simons Island, GA to Amelia Island, FL.

(a) A line drawn from St. Simons Light to the northernmost tank on Jekyll Island charted in approximate position latitude 31°05.9' N., longitude 81° 24.5' W.

(b) A line drawn from the southernmost tank on Jekyll Island charted in approximate position latitude 31°01.6' N., longitude 81°25.2' W., to coordinate latitude 30°59.4' N., longitude 81°23.7' W., (0.5 nautical mile east of the charted position of St. Andrew Sound Lighted Buoy 32); thence to the abandoned lighthouse tower on the north end of Little Cumberland Island charted in approximate position latitude 30°58.5' N., longitude 81°24.8' W.

(c) A line drawn across the seaward extremity of the St. Marys Entrance Jetties.

§ 80.723 Amelia Island, FL to Cape Canaveral, FL.

(a) A line drawn from the southernmost extremity of Amelia Island to the northeasternmost extremity of Little Talbot Island.

(b) A line formed by the centerline of the highway bridge from Little Talbot Island to Fort George Island.

(c) A line drawn across the seaward extremity of the St. Johns River Entrance Jetties.

(d) A line drawn across the seaward extremity of the St. Augustine Inlet Jetties.

(e) A line formed by the centerline of the highway bridge over Matanzas Inlet.

(f) A line drawn across the seaward extremity of the Ponce de Leon Inlet Jetties.

§ 80.727 Cape Canaveral, FL to Miami Beach, FL.

(a) A line drawn across the seaward extremity of the Port Canaveral Entrance Channel Jetties.

(b) A line drawn across the seaward extremity of the Sebastian Inlet Jetties.

(c) A line drawn across the seaward extremity of the Fort Pierce Inlet Jetties.

(d) A north-south line (longitude 80° 09.7' W.) drawn across St. Lucie Inlet.

(e) A line drawn from the seaward extremity of Jupiter Inlet North Jetty to the northeast extremity of the concrete apron on the south side of Jupiter inlet.

(f) A line drawn across the seaward extremity of the Lake Worth Inlet Jetties.

(g) A line drawn across the seaward extremity of the Boynton Inlet Jetties.

(h) A line drawn from Boca Raton Inlet North Jetty Light 2 to Boca Raton Inlet South Jetty Light 1.

(i) A line drawn from Hillsboro Inlet Light to Hillsboro Inlet Entrance Light 2; thence to Hillsboro Inlet Entrance Light 1; thence west to the shoreline.

(j) A line drawn across the seaward extremity of the Port Everglades Entrance Jetties.

(k) A line formed by the centerline of the highway bridge over Bakers Haulover Inlet.

§ 80.730 Miami Harbor, FL.

A line drawn across the seaward extremity of the Miami Harbor Government Cut Jetties.

§ 80.735 Miami, FL to Long Key, FL.

(a) A line drawn from the southernmost extremity of Fisher Island 212° true to the point latitude 25°45.0' N., longitude 80° 08.6' W., on Virginia Key.

(b) A line formed by the centerline of the highway bridge between Virginia Key and Key Biscayne.

(c) A line drawn from Cape Florida Light to the northern most extremity on Soldier Key.

(d) A line drawn from the southernmost extremity on Soldier Key to the northernmost extremity of the Ragged Keys.

(e) A line drawn from the Ragged Keys to the southernmost extremity of Angelfish Key following the general trend of the seaward shoreline.

(f) A line drawn on the centerline of the Overseas Highway (U.S. 1) and bridges from latitude 25°19.3' N., longitude 80°16.0' W., at Little Angelfish Creek to the radar dome charted on Long Key at approximate position latitude 24°49.3' N., longitude 80°49.2' W.

CARIBBEAN ISLANDS

SEVENTH DISTRICT

§ 80.738 Puerto Rico and Virgin Islands.

(a) Except inside lines specifically described in this section, the 72 COLREGS shall apply on all other bays, harbors and lagoons of Puerto Rico and the U.S. Virgin Islands.

(b) A line drawn from Puerto San Juan Light to position 18°28.5' N., 066°08.4' W, at the northwest extent of Isla de Cabras across the entrance of San Juan Harbor.

GULF COAST

SEVENTH DISTRICT

§ 80.740 Long Key, FL to Cape Sable, FL.

A line drawn from the microwave tower charted on Long Key at approximate position latitude 24° 48.8' N., longitude 80° 49.6' W., to Long Key Light 1; thence to Arsenic Bank Light 2; thence to Sprigger Bank Light 5; thence to Schooner Bank Light 6; thence to Oxfoot Bank Light 10; thence to East Cape Light 2; thence through East Cape Daybeacon 1A to the shoreline at East Cape.

§ 80.745 Cape Sable, FL to Cape Romano, FL.

(a) A line drawn following the general trend of the mainland, highwater shoreline from Cape Sable at East Cape to Little Shark River Light 1; thence to westernmost extremity of Shark Point; thence following the general trend of the mainland, highwater shoreline crossing the entrances of Harney River, Broad Creek, Broad River, Rodgers River First Bay, Chatham River, Huston River, to the shoreline at coordinate latitude 25°41.8' N., longitude 81°17.9' W.

(b) The 72 COLREGS shall apply to the waters surrounding the Ten Thousand Islands and the bays, creeks, inlets, and rivers between Chatham Bend and Marco Island except inside lines specifically described in this part.

(c) A north-south line drawn at longitude 81°20.2' W., across the entrance to Lopez River.

(d) A line drawn across the entrance to Turner River parallel to the general trend of the shoreline.

(e) A line formed by the centerline of Highway 92 Bridge at Goodland.

§ 80.748 Cape Romano, FL to Sanibel Island, FL.

(a) A line drawn across Big Marco Pass parallel to the general trend of the seaward, highwater shoreline.

(b) A line drawn from the northwesternmost extremity of Coconut Island 000°T across Capri Pass.

(c) Lines drawn across Hurricane and Little Marco Passes parallel to the general trend of the seaward, highwater shoreline.

(d) A line from the seaward extremity of Gordon Pass South Jetty 014° true to the shoreline at approximate coordinate latitude 26°05.7' N., longitude 81°48.1' W.

(e) A line drawn across the seaward extremity of Doctors Pass Jetties.

(f) Lines drawn across Wiggins, Big Hickory, New, and Big Carlos Passes parallel to the general trend of the seaward highwater *shoreline.*

(g) A straight line drawn from Sanibel Island Light through Matanzas Pass Channel Light 2 to the shore of Estero Island.

§ 80.750 Sanibel Island, FL to St. Petersburg, FL.

(a) A line formed by the centerline of the highway bridge over Blind Pass, between Captiva Island and Sanibel Island, and lines drawn across Redfish and Captiva Passes parallel to the general trend of the seaward, highwater shorelines.

(b) A line drawn from La Costa Test Pile North Light to Port Boca Grande Light.

(c) Lines drawn across Gasparilla and Stump Passes parallel to the general trend of the seaward, highwater shorelines.

(d) A line across the seaward extremity of Venice Inlet Jetties.

(e) A line drawn across Midnight Pass parallel to the general trend of the seaward, highwater shoreline.

(f) A line drawn from Big Sarasota Pass Light 14 to the southernmost extremity of Lido Key.

(g) A line drawn across New Pass tangent to the seaward, highwater shoreline of Longboat Key.

(h) A line drawn across Longboat Pass parallel to the seaward, highwater shoreline.

(i) A line drawn from the northwesternmost extremity of Bean Point to the southeasternmost extremity of Egmont Key.

(j) A straight line drawn from Egmont Key Light through Egmont Channel Range Rear Light to the shoreline on Mullet Key.

(k) A line drawn from the northernmost extremity of Mullet Key across Bunces Pass and South Channel to Pass-a-Grille Channel Light 8; thence to Pass-a-Grille Channel Daybeacon 9; thence to the southwesternmost extremity of Long Key.

§ 80.753 St. Petersburg, FL to the Anclote, FL.

(a) A line drawn across Blind Pass, between Treasure Island and Long Key, parallel with the general trend of the seaward, highwater shoreline.

(b) Lines formed by the centerline of the highway bridges over Johns and Clearwater Passes.

(c) A line drawn across Dunedin and Hurricane Passes parallel with the general trend of the seaward, highwater shoreline.

(d) A line drawn from the northernmost extremity of Honeymoon Island to Anclote Anchorage South Entrance Light 7; thence to Anclote Key 28°10.0' N., 82°50.6' W; thence a straight line through Anclote River Cut B Range Rear Light to the shoreline.

§ 80.755 Anclote, FL to the Suncoast Keys, FL.

(a) Except inside lines specifically described in this section, the 72 COLREGS shall apply on the bays, bayous, creeks, marinas, and rivers from Anclote to the Suncoast Keys.

(b) A north-south line drawn at longitude 82°38.3' W., across the Chassahowitzka River Entrance.

§ 80.757 Suncoast Keys, FL to Horseshoe Point, FL.

(a) Except inside lines specifically described in this section, the 72 COLREGS shall apply on the bays, bayous, creeks, and marinas from the Suncoast Keys to Horseshoe Point.

(b) A line formed by the centerline of Highway 44 Bridge over the Salt River.

(c) A north-south line drawn through Crystal River Entrance Daybeacon 25 across the river entrance.

(d) A north-south line drawn through the Cross Florida Barge Canal Daybeacon 48 across the canal.

(e) A north-south line drawn through Withlacoochee River Daybeacon 40 across the river.

(f) A line drawn from the westernmost extremity of South Point north to the shoreline across the Waccasassa River Entrance.

(g) A line drawn from position latitude 29°16.6' N., longitude 83°06.7' W., 300° true to the shoreline of Hog Island.

(h) A north-south line drawn through Suwannee River Mcgriff Pass Daybeacons 30 and 31 across the Suwannee River.

§ 80.760 Horseshoe Point, FL to Rock Islands, FL.

(a) Except inside lines specifically described provided in this section, the 72 COLREGS shall apply on the bays, bayous, creeks, marinas, and rivers from Horseshoe Point to the Rock Islands.

(b) A north-south line drawn through Steinhatchee River Light 21.

(c) A line drawn from Fenholloway River Approach Light FR east across the entrance to Fenholloway River.

§ 80.805 Rock Island, FL to Cape San Blas, FL.

(a) A north-south line drawn from the Econfina River Light to the opposite shore.

(b) A line drawn from Gamble Point Light to the southernmost extremity of Cabell Point.

(c) A line drawn from St. Marks Range Rear Light to St. Marks Channel Light 11; thence to the southernmost extremity of Live Oak Point; thence in a straight line through Shell Point Light to the southernmost extremity of Ochlockonee Point; thence to Bald Point along longitude 84°20.5' W.

(d) A line drawn from the south shore of Southwest Cape at longitude 84°22.7' W., to Dog Island Reef East Light 1; thence a straight line to the easternmost extremity of Dog Island.

(e) A line drawn from the westernmost extremity of Dog Island to the easternmost extremity of St. George Island.

(f) A line drawn across the seaward extremity of the St. George Island Channel Jetties.

(g) A line drawn from the northwesternmost extremity of Sand Island to West Pass Light 7.

(h) A line drawn from the westernmost extremity of St. Vincent Island to the southeast, highwater shoreline of Indian Peninsula at longitude 85°13.5' W.

§ 80.810 Cape San Blas, FL to Perdido Bay, FL.

(a) A line drawn from St. Joseph Bay Entrance Range A Rear Light through St. Joseph Bay Entrance Range B Front Light to St. Joseph Point.

(b) A line drawn across the mouth of Salt Creek as an extension of the general trend of the shoreline to continue across the inlet to St. Andrews Sound in the middle of Crooked Island.

(c) A line drawn from the northernmost extremity of Crooked Island 000° T. to the mainland.

(d) A line drawn from the easternmost extremity of Shell Island 120° to the shoreline across the east entrance to St. Andrews Bay.

(e) A line drawn between the seaward end of the St. Andrews Bay Entrance Jetties.

(f) A line drawn between the seaward end of the Choctawatchee Bay Entrance Jetties.

(g) An east-west line drawn from Fort McRee Leading Light across the Pensacola Bay Entrance along latitude 30°19.5' N.

(h) A line drawn between the seaward end of the Perdido Pass Jetties.

§ 80.815 Mobile Bay, AL to the Chandeleur Islands, LA.

(a) A line drawn across the in lets to Little Lagoon as an extension of the general trend of the shoreline.

(b) A line drawn from 30°14'41.4" N., 088°01'26.5" W. (Mobile Point Light) to 30°15'13.3" N., 088°03'22.6" W. (Dauphin Island Channel Light 1) to the eastern corner of Fort Gaines at Pelican Point. A line drawn from the westernmost extremity of Dauphin Island to the easternmost extremity of Petit Bois Island.

(c) A line drawn from Horn Island Pass Entrance Range Front Light on Petit Bois Island to the easternmost extremity of Horn Island.

(d) An east-west line (latitude 30°14.7' N.) drawn between the westernmost extremity of Horn Island to the easternmost extremity of Ship Island.

(e) A curved line drawn following the general trend of the seaward, highwater shoreline of Ship Island.

(f) A line drawn from Ship Island Light to Chandeleur Light; thence in a curved line following the general trend of the seaward, highwater shorelines of the Chandeleur Islands to the island at latitude 29°44.1' N., longitude 88°53.0' W.; thence to latitude 29°26.5' N., longitude 88° 55.6' W.

§ 80.825 Mississippi Passes, LA.

(a) A line drawn from latitude 29°26.5' N., longitude 88°55.6' W. to latitude 29°10.6' N., longitude 88°59.8' W.; thence to latitude 29°03.5' N., longitude 89°03.7' W.; thence to latitude 28°58.8' N., longitude 89°04.3' W.

(b) A line drawn from latitude 28°58.8' N., longitude 89°04.3' W.; to latitude 28°57.3' N., longitude 89°05.3' W.; thence to latitude 28°56.95' N., longitude 89°05.6' W.; thence to latitude 29°00.4' N., longitude 89°09.8' W.; thence following the general trend of the seaward highwater shoreline in a northwesterly direction to latitude 29°03.4' N., longitude 89°13.0' W.; thence west to latitude 29°03.5' N., longitude 89°15.5' W.; thence following the general trend of the seaward high water shoreline in a southwesterly direction to latitude 28°57.7' N., longitude 89°22.3' W.

(c) A line drawn from latitude 28°57.7' N., longitude 89°22.3' W.; to latitude 28°51.4' N., longitude 89°24.5' W.; thence to latitude 28°52.65' N., longitude 89°27.1' W.; thence to the seaward extremity of the Southwest Pass West Jetty located at latitude 28°54.5' N., longitude 89°26.1' W.

§ 80.830 Mississippi Passes, LA to Point Au Fer, LA.

(a) A line drawn from the seaward extremity of the Southwest Pass West Jetty located at coordinate latitude 28°54.5' N., longitude 89°26.1' W.; thence following the general trend of the seaward, highwater jetty and shoreline in a north, northeasterly direction to Old Tower latitude 28°58.8' N., longitude 89°23.3' W.; thence to westernmost point near Pass du Bois; thence to coordinate latitude 29°05.2' N., longitude 89°24.3' W.; thence a curved line following the general trend of the highwater shoreline to Point Au Fer Island except as otherwise described in this section.

(b) A line drawn across the seaward extremity of the Empire Waterway (Bayou Fontanelle) entrance jetties.

(c) An east-west line drawn from the westernmost extremity of Grand Terre Islands in the direction of 194° true to the Grand Isle Fishing Jetty Light.

(d) A line drawn between the seaward extremity of the Belle Pass Jetties.

(e) A line drawn from the westernmost extremity of the Timbalier Island to the easternmost extremity of Isles Dernieres.

(f) A north-south line drawn from Caillou Bay Light 13 across Caillou Boca.

(g) A line drawn 107° true from Caillou Bay Boat Landing Light across the entrances to Grand Bayou du Large and Bayou Grand Caillou.

(h) A line drawn on an axis of 103° true through Taylors Bayou Entrance Light 2 across the entrances to Jack Stout Bayou, Taylors Bayou, Pelican Pass, and Bayou de West.

§ 80.835 Point Au Fer, LA to Calcasieu Pass, LA.

(a) A line drawn from Point Au Fer to Atchafalaya Channel Light 34; thence to Atchafalaya Channel Light 33; thence to Atchafalaya Bay Pipeline Light D latitude 29°25.0' N., longitude 91°31.7' W.; thence to Atchafalaya Bay Light 1 latitude 29°25.3' N., longitude 91°35.8' W.; thence to South Point.

(b) Lines following the general trend of the highwater shoreline drawn across the bayou and canal inlets from the Gulf of Mexico between South Point and Calcasieu Pass except as otherwise described in this section.

(c) A line drawn on an axis of 140° true through Southwest Pass Vermillion Bay Light 4 across Southwest Pass.

(d) A line drawn across the seaward extremity of the Freshwater Bayou Canal Entrance Jetties.

(e) A line drawn from Mermentau Channel East Jetty Light 6 to Mermentau Channel West Jetty Light 7.

(f) A line drawn from the radio tower charted in approximate position latitude 29°45.7' N., longitude 93°06.3' W., 115° true across Mermentau Pass.

(g) A line drawn across the seaward extremity of the Calcasieu Pass Jetties.

§ 80.840 Sabine Pass, TX to Galveston, TX.

(a) A line drawn from the Sabine Pass East Jetty Light to the seaward end of the Sabine Pass West Jetty.

(b) A line drawn across the small boat passes through the Sabine Pass East and West Jetties.

(c) A line formed by the centerline of the highway bridge over Rollover Pass at Gilchrist.

§ 80.845 Galveston, TX to Freeport, TX.

(a) A line drawn from Galveston North Jetty Light 6A to Galveston South Jetty Light 5A.

(b) A line formed by the centerline of the highway bridge over San Luis Pass.

(c) Lines formed by the centerlines of the highway bridges over the inlets to Christmas Bay (Cedar Cut) and Drum Bay.

(d) A line drawn from the seaward extremity of the Freeport North Jetty to Freeport Entrance Light 6; thence to Freeport Entrance Light 7; thence to the seaward extremity of Freeport South Jetty.

§ 80.850 Brazos River, TX to the Rio Grande, TX.

(a) Except as otherwise described in this section lines drawn continuing the general trend of the seaward, highwater shorelines across the inlets to Brazos River Diversion Channel, San Bernard River, Cedar Lakes, Brown Cedar Cut, Colorado River, Matagorda Bay, Cedar Bayou, Corpus Christi Bay, and Laguna Madre.

(b) A line drawn across the seaward extremity of Matagorda Ship Channel North Jetties.

(c) A line drawn from the seaward tangent of Matagorda Peninsula at Decros Point to Matagorda Light.

(d) A line drawn across the seaward extremity of the Aransas Pass Jetties.

(e) A line drawn across the seaward extremity of the Port Mansfield Entrance Jetties.

(f) A line drawn across the seaward extremity of the Brazos Santiago Pass Jetties.

PACIFIC COAST

ELEVENTH DISTRICT

§ 80.1102 Santa Catalina Island, CA.

The 72 COLREGS shall apply to the harbors on Santa Catalina Island.

§ 80.1104 San Diego Harbor, CA.

A line drawn from Zuniga Jetty Light "V" to Zuniga Jetty Light "Z"; thence to Point Loma Light.

§ 80.1106 Mission Bay, CA.

A line drawn from Mission Bay South Jetty Light 2 to Mission Bay North Jetty Light 1.

§ 80.1108 Oceanside Harbor, CA.

A line drawn from Oceanside South Jetty Light 4 to Oceanside Breakwater Light 3.

§ 80.1110 Dana Point Harbor, CA.

A line drawn from Dana Point Jetty Light 4 to Dana Point Breakwater Light 3.

§ 80.1112 Newport Bay, CA.

A line drawn from Newport Bay East Jetty Light 4 to Newport Bay West Jetty Light 3.

§ 80.1114 San Pedro Bay- Anaheim Bay, CA.

(a) A line drawn across the seaward extremities of the Anaheim Bay Entrance East Jetties; thence to Long Beach Breakwater East End Light 1.

(b) A line drawn from Long Beach Channel Entrance Light 2 to Long Beach Light.

(c) A line drawn from Los Angeles Main Entrance Channel Light 2 to Los Angeles Light.

§ 80.1116 Redondo Harbor, CA.

A line drawn from Redondo Beach East Jetty Light 2 to Redondo Beach West Jetty Light 3.

§ 80.1118 Marina Del Rey, CA.

(a) A line drawn from Marina Del Rey Breakwater South Light 1 to Marina Del Rey Light 4.

(b) A line drawn from Marina Del Rey Breakwater North Light 2 to Marina Del Rey Light 3.

(c) A line drawn from Marina Del Rey Light 4 to the seaward extremity of the Ballona Creek South Jetty.

§ 80.1120 Port Hueneme, CA.

A line drawn from Port Hueneme East Jetty Light 4 to Port Hueneme West Jetty Light 3.

§ 80.1122 Channel Islands Harbor, CA.

(a) A line drawn from Channel Islands Harbor South Jetty Light 2 to Channel Islands Harbor Breakwater South Light 1.

(b) A line drawn from Channel Islands Harbor Breakwater North Light to Channel Islands Harbor North Jetty Light 5.

§ 80.1124 Ventura Marina, CA.

A line drawn from Ventura Marina South Jetty Light 6 to Ventura Marina Breakwater South Light 3; thence to Ventura Marina North Jetty Light 7.

§ 80.1126 Santa Barbara Harbor, CA.

A line drawn from Santa Barbara Harbor Light 4 to Santa Barbara Harbor Breakwater Light.

§ 80.1130 San Luis Obispo Bay, CA.

A line drawn from the southernmost extremity of Fossil Point to the seaward extremity of Whaler Island Breakwater.

§ 80.1132 Estero-Morro Bay, CA.

A line drawn from the seaward extremity of the Morro Bay East Breakwater to the Morro Bay West Breakwater Light.

§ 80.1134 Monterey Harbor, CA.

A line drawn from Monterey Harbor Light 6 to the northern extremity of Monterey Municipal Wharf 2.

§ 80.1136 Moss Landing Harbor, CA.

A line drawn from the seaward extremity of the pier located 0.3 mile south of Moss Landing Harbor Entrance to the seaward extremity of the Moss Landing Harbor North Breakwater.

§ 80.1138 Santa Cruz Harbor, CA.

A line drawn from the seaward extremity of the Santa Cruz Harbor East Breakwater to Santa Cruz Harbor West Breakwater Light; thence to Santa Cruz Light.

§ 80.1140 Pillar Point Harbor, CA.

A line drawn from Pillar Point Harbor Light 6 to Pillar Point Harbor Entrance Light.

§ 80.1142 San Francisco Harbor, CA.

A straight line drawn from Point Bonita Light through Mile Rocks Light to the shore.

§ 80.1144 Bodega and Tomales Bay, CA.

(a) An east-west line drawn from Sand Point to Avalis Beach.

(b) A line drawn from the seaward extremity of Bodega Harbor North Breakwater to Bodega Harbor Entrance Light 1.

§ 80.1146 Albion River, CA.

A line drawn on an axis of 030° true through Albion River Light 1 across Albion Cove.

§ 80.1148 Noyo River, CA.

A line drawn from Noyo River Entrance Daybeacon 4 to Noyo River Entrance Light 5.

§ 80.1150 Arcata-Humboldt Bay, CA.

A line drawn from Humboldt Bay Entrance Light 4 to Humboldt Bay Entrance Light 3.

§ 80.1152 Crescent City Harbor, CA.

A line drawn from Crescent City Entrance Light to the southeasternmost extremity of Whaler Island.

THIRTEENTH DISTRICT

§ 80.1305 Chetco River, OR.

A line drawn across the seaward extremities of the Chetco River Entrance Jetties.

§ 80.1310 Rogue River, OR.

A line drawn across the seaward extremities of the Rogue River Entrance Jetties.

§ 80.1315 Coquille River, OR.

A line drawn across the seaward extremities of the Coquille River Entrance Jetties.

§ 80.1320 Coos Bay, OR.

A line drawn across the seaward extremities of the Coos Bay Entrance Jetties.

§ 80.1325 Umpqua River, OR.

A line drawn across the seaward extremities of the Umpqua Entrance Jetties.

§ 80.1330 Siuslaw River, OR.

A line drawn across the seaward extremities of the Siuslaw River Entrance Jetties.

§ 80.1335 Alsea Bay, OR.

A line drawn from the seaward shoreline on the north of the Alsea Bay Entrance 165° true across the channel entrance.

§ 80.1340 Yaquina Bay, OR.

A line drawn across the seaward extremities of Yaquina Bay Entrance Jetties.

§ 80.1345 Depoe Bay, OR.

A line drawn across the Depoe Bay Channel entrance parallel with the general trend of the highwater shoreline.

§ 80.1350 Netarts Bay, OR.

A line drawn from the northernmost extremity of the shore on the south side of Netarts Bay north to the opposite shoreline.

§ 80.1355 Tillamook Bay, OR.

A line drawn across the seaward extremities of the Tillamook Bay Entrance Jetties.

§ 80.1360 Nehalem River, OR.

A line drawn approximately parallel with the general trend of the highwater shoreline across the Nehalem River Entrance.

§ 80.1365 Columbia River Entrance, OR/WA.

A line drawn from the seaward extremity of the Columbia River North Jetty (above water) 155° true to the seaward extremity of the Columbia River South Jetty (above water).

§ 80.1370 Willapa Bay, WA.

A line drawn from Willapa Bay Light 169.8° true to the westernmost tripod charted 1.6 miles south of Leadbetter Point.

§ 80.1375 Grays Harbor, WA.

A line drawn across the seaward extremities (above water) of the Grays Harbor Entrance Jetties.

§ 80.1380 Quillayute River, WA.

A line drawn from the seaward extremity of the Quillayute River Entrance East Jetty to the overhead power cable tower charted on James Island; thence a straight line through Quillayute River Entrance Light 3 to the shoreline.

§ 80.1385 Strait of Juan de Fuca.

The 72 COLREGS shall apply on all waters of the Strait of Juan de Fuca.

§ 80.1390 Haro Strait and Strait of Georgia.

The 72 COLREGS shall apply on all waters of the Haro Strait and the Strait of Georgia.

§ 80.1395 Puget Sound and Adjacent Waters.

The 72 COLREGS shall apply on all waters of Puget Sound and adjacent waters, including Lake Union, Lake Washington, Hood Canal, and all tributaries.

PACIFIC ISLANDS

FOURTEENTH DISTRICT

§ 80.1410 Hawaiian Island Exemption from General Rule.

Except as provided elsewhere in this part for Mamala Bay and Kaneohe Bay on Oahu; Port Allen and Nawiliwili Bay on Kauai; Kahului Harbor on Maui; and Kawailae and Hilo Harbors on Hawaii, the 72 COLREGS shall apply on all other bays, harbors, and lagoons of the Hawaiian Island (including Midway).

§ 80.1420 Mamala Bay, Oahu, HI.

A line drawn from 21°17'46.9" N., 158°06'22.2" W. (Barbers Point Light), 21°15'20.5" N., 157°48'34.3" W. (Diamond Head Light).

§ 80.1430 Kaneohe Bay, Oahu, HI.

A line drawn from 21°27'44.1" N., 157°45'48.6" W. (Pyramid Rock Light), across Kaneohe Bay through the center of Mokolii Island to the shoreline.

§ 80.1440 Port Allen, Kauai, HI.

A line drawn from 21°53'34.3" N., 159°36'15.6" W. (Puolo Point Light) to 21°53'49.0"N., 159°35'27.2"W. (Hanapepe Breakwater Light 2).

§ 80.1450 Nawiliwili Harbor, Kauai, HI.

A line drawn from the seaward extremity of Nawiliwili Harbor breakwater to 21°57'23.8" N., 159°20'52.7" W. (Kukii Point Light).

§ 80.1460 Kahului Harbor, Maui, HI.

A line drawn from 20°54'04.1" N., 156°28'26.8" W. (Kahului Entrance Breakwater Light 4), to 20°54'02.3" N., 156°28'26.8" W. (Kahului Entrance Breakwater Light 4).

§ 80.1470 Kawaihae Harbor, Hawaii, HI.

A line drawn from 20°02'29.1" N., 155°49'58.2" W. (Kawaihae Light), to the seaward extremity of the Kawaihae South Breakwater.

§ 80.1480 Hilo Harbor, Hawaii, HI.

A line drawn from the seaward extremity of the Hilo Breakwater 265° true (as an extension of the seaward side of the breakwater) to the shoreline 0.2 nautical mile north of Alealea Point.

§ 80.1490 Apra Harbor, U.S. Territory of Guam.

A line drawn from the westernmost extremity of Orote Island to the westernmost extremity of Glass Breakwater.

§ 80.1495 U.S. Pacific Island Possessions.

The 72 COLREGS shall apply on the bays, harbors, lagoons, and waters surrounding the U.S. Pacific Island Possessions of American Samoa, Baker, Howland, Jarvis, Johnson, Palmyra, Swains and Wake Island.

ALASKA

SEVENTEENTH DISTRICT

§ 80.1705 Alaska

The 72 COLREGS shall apply on all the sounds, bays, harbors, and inlets of Alaska.

OPERATIONS OF VESSELS GENERALLY
46 U.S.C. 2301-2307

§ 2301 Application

Except as provided in sections 2304 and 2306 of this title, this chapter applies to a vessel operated on waters subject to the jurisdiction of the United States (including the territorial sea of the United States as described in Presidential Proclamation No. 5928 of December 27. 1988) and, for a vessel owned in the United States, on the high seas.

§ 2302 Penalties for negligent operations and interfering with safe operations

(a) A person operating a vessel in a negligent manner or interfering with the safe operation of a vessel so as to endanger the life, limb, or property of a person is liable to the United States Government for a civil penalty of not more than $5,000 in the case of a recreational vessel or $25,000 in the case of any other vessel.

(b) A person operating a vessel in a grossly negligent manner that endangers the life, limb, or property of a person commits a class A misdemeanor.

(c) An individual who is under the influence of alcohol, or a dangerous drug in violation of a law of the United States when operating a vessel, as determined under standards prescribed by the Secretary by regulation—

(1) is liable to the United States Government for a civil penalty of not more than $5,000; or

(2) commits a class A misdemeanor.

(d) For a penalty imposed under this section, the vessel also is liable in rem unless the vessel is—

(1) owned by a State or a political subdivision of a State;

(2) operated principally for governmental purposes; and

(3) identified clearly as a vessel of that State or subdivision.

(e) (1) A vessel may not transport Government-impelled cargoes if –

(A) the vessel has been detained and determined to be substandard by the Secretary for violation of an international safety convention to which the United States is a party, and the Secretary has published notice of the detention and determination in an electronic form, including the name of the owner of the vessel; or

(B) the operator of the vessel has on more than one occasion had a vessel detained and determined to be substandard by the Secretary for violation of an international safety convention to which the United States is a party, and the Secretary has published notice of the detention and determination in an electronic form, including the name of the owner of the vessel.

(2) The prohibition in paragraph (1) expires for a vessel on the earlier of –

(A) 1 year after the date of the publication in electronic form on which the prohibition is based; or

(B) any date on which the owner or operator of the vessel prevails in an appeal of the violation of the relevant international convention on which the detention is based.

(3) As used in this subsection, the term "Government-impelled cargo" means cargo for which a Federal agency contracts directly for shipping by water or for which (or the freight of which) a Federal agency provides the financing, including financing by grant, loan or loan guarantee, resulting in shipment of the cargo by water.

§ 2303 Duties related to marine casualty assistance and information

(a) The master or individual in charge of a vessel involved in a marine casualty shall—

(1) render necessary assistance to each individual affected to save that affected individual from danger caused by the marine casualty, so far as the master or individual in charge can do so without serious danger to the master's or individual's vessel or to individuals on board; and

(2) give the master's or individual's name and address and identification of the vessel to the master or individual in charge of any other vessel involved in the casualty, to any individual injured, and to the owner of any property damaged.

(b) An individual violating this section or a regulation prescribed under this section shall be fined not more than $1,000 or imprisoned for not more than 2 years. The vessel also is liable in rem to the United States Government for the fine.

(c) An individual complying with subsection (a) of this section or gratuitously and in good faith rendering assistance at the scene of a marine casualty without objection by an individual assisted, is not liable for damages as a result of rendering assistance or for an act or omission in providing or arranging salvage, towage, medical treatment, or other assistance when the individual acts as an ordinary, reasonable, and prudent individual would have acted under the circumstances.

OPERATIONS OF VESSELS—CONTINUED

§ 2303a Post serious marine casualty alcohol testing

(a) The Secretary shall establish procedures to ensure that after a serious marine casualty occurs, alcohol testing of crew members or other persons responsible for the operation of other safety-sensitive functions of the vessel or vessels involved in such casualty is conducted no later than 2 hours after the casualty occurs, unless such testing cannot be completed within that time due to safety concerns directly related to the casualty.

(b) The procedures in subsection (a) shall require that if alcohol testing cannot be completed within 2 hours of the occurrence of the casualty, such testing shall be conducted as soon thereafter as the safety concerns in subsection (a) have been adequately addressed to permit such testing, except that such testing may not be required more than 8 hours after the casualty occurs.

§ 2304 Duty to provide assistance at sea

(a) (1) A master or individual in charge of a vessel shall render assistance to any individual found at sea in danger of being lost, so far as the master or individual in charge can do so without serious danger to the master's or individual's vessel or individuals on board.

(2) Paragraph (1) does not apply to a vessel of war or a vessel owned by the United States Government appropriated only to a public service.

(b) A master or individual violating this section shall be fined not more than $1,000, imprisoned for not more than 2 years, or both.

§ 2305 Injunctions

(a) The district courts of the United States have jurisdiction to enjoin the negligent operation of vessels prohibited by this chapter on the petition of the Attorney General for the United States Government.

(b) When practicable, the Secretary shall—

(1) give notice to any person against whom an action for injunctive relief is considered under this section an opportunity to present that person's views; and

(2) except for a knowing and willful violation, give the person a reasonable opportunity to achieve compliance.

(c) The failure to give notice and opportunity to present views under subsection (b) of this section does not preclude the court from granting appropriate relief.

Vessel Traffic Service Area or VTS Area means the geographical area encompassing a specific VTS area of service as described in Part 161 of this chapter. This area of service may be subdivided into sectors for the purpose of allocating responsibility to individual Vessel Traffic Centers or to identify different operating requirements.

Note: Although regulatory jurisdiction is limited to the navigable waters of the United States, certain vessels will be encouraged or may be required, as a condition of port entry, to report beyond this area to facilitate traffic management within the VTS area.

(Rule 1, International Regulations for Preventing Collisions at Sea, 1972 (as rectified); EO 11964 (14 U.S.C. 2); 49 CFR 1.46(b))

§ 26.03 Radiotelephone required.

(a) Unless an exemption is granted under §26.09 and except as provided in paragraph (a)(4) of this section, this part applies to:

(1) Every power-driven vessel of 20 meters or over in length while navigating;

(2) Every vessel of 100 gross tons and upward carrying one or more passengers for hire while navigating;

(3) Every towing vessel of 26 feet or over in length while navigating; and

(4) Every dredge and floating plant engaged in or near a channel or fairway in operations likely to restrict or affect navigation of other vessels except for an unmanned or intermittently manned floating plant under the control of a dredge.

(b) Every vessel, dredge, or floating plant described in paragraph (a) of this section must have a radiotelephone on board capable of operation from its navigational bridge, or in the case of a dredge, from its main control station, and capable of transmitting and receiving on the frequency or frequencies within the 156-162 Mega-Hertz band using the classes of emissions designated by the Federal Communications Commission for the exchange of navigational information.

(c) The radiotelephone required by paragraph (b) of this section must be carried on board the described vessels, dredges, and floating plants upon the navigable waters of the United States.

(d) The radiotelephone required by paragraph (b) of this section must be capable of transmitting and receiving on VHF FM channel 22A (157.1 MHz).

(e) While transiting any of the following waters, each vessel described in paragraph (a) of this section also must have on board a radiotelephone capable of transmitting and receiving on VHF FM channel 67 (156.375 MHz):

(1) The lower Mississippi River from the territorial sea boundary, and within either the Southwest Pass safety fairway or the South Pass safety fairway specified in 33 CFR 166.200, to mile 242.4 AHP (Above Head of Passes) near Baton Rouge;

(2) The Mississippi River-Gulf Outlet from the territorial sea boundary, and within the Mississippi River-Gulf Outlet Safety Fairway specified in 33 CFR 166.200, to that channel's junction with the Inner Harbor Navigation Canal; and

(3) The full length of the Inner Harbor Navigation Canal from its junction with the Mississippi River to that canal's entry to Lake Pontchartrain at the New Seabrook vehicular bridge.

(f) In addition to the radiotelephone required by paragraph (b) of this section, each vessel described in paragraph (a) of this section while transiting any waters within a Vessel Traffic Service Area, must have on board a radiotelephone capable of transmitting and receiving on the VTS designated frequency in Table 161.12(c) (VTS and VMRS Center, Call Signs/MMSI, Designated Frequencies, and Monitoring Areas).

Note: A single VHF FM radio capable of scanning or sequential monitoring (often referred to as "dual watch" capability) will not meet the requirements for two radios.

§ 26.04 Use of the designated frequency.

(a) No person may use the frequency designated by the Federal Communications Commission under section 8 of the Act, 33 U.S.C. 1207(a), to transmit any information other than information necessary for the safe navigation of vessels or necessary tests.

(b) Each person who is required to maintain a listening watch under section 5 of the Act shall, when necessary, transmit and confirm, on the designated frequency, the intentions of his vessel and any other information necessary for the safe navigation of vessels.

(c) Nothing in these regulations may be construed as prohibiting the use of the designated frequency to communicate with shore stations to obtain or furnish information necessary for the safe navigation of vessels.

(d) On the navigable waters of the United States, channel 13 (156.65 MHz) is the designated frequency required to be monitored in accordance with §26.05(a) except that in the area prescribed in §26.03(e), channel 67 (156.375 MHz) is an additional frequency.

(e) On those navigable waters of the United States within a VTS area, the designated VTS frequency is the designated frequency required to be monitored[‡] in accordance with §26.05.

[‡] Per 47 CFR 80.148(b), a VHF watch on Channel 16 (156.800 MHz) is not required on vessels subject to the Vessel Bridge-to-Bridge Radiotelephone Act and participating in a Vessel Traffic Service (VTS) system when the watch is maintained on both the vessel bridge-to-bridge frequency and a designated VTS frequency.

§ 26.05 Use of Radiotelephone.

Section 5 of the Act states that the radiotelephone required by this Act is for the exclusive use of the master or person in charge of the vessel, or the person designated by the master or person in charge to pilot or direct the movement of the vessel, who shall maintain a listening watch on the designated frequency. Nothing herein shall be interpreted as precluding the use of portable radiotelephone equipment to satisfy the requirements of this Act.

§ 26.06 Maintenance of radiotelephone; failure of radiotelephone.

Section 6 of the Act states:

(a) Whenever radiotelephone capability is required by this Act, a vessel's radiotelephone equipment shall be maintained in effective operating condition. If the radiotelephone equipment carried aboard a vessel ceases to operate, the master shall exercise due diligence to restore it or cause it to be restored to effective operating condition at the earliest practicable time. The failure of a vessel's radiotelephone equipment shall not, in itself, constitute a violation of this Act, nor shall it obligate the master of any vessel to moor or anchor his vessel; however, the loss of radiotelephone capability shall be given consideration in the navigation of the vessel.

§ 26.07 Communications.

No person may use the services of, and no person may serve as, a person required to maintain a listening watch under section 5 of the Act, 33 U.S.C. 1204, unless the person can communicate in the English language.

§ 26.08 Exemption procedures.

(a) The Commandant has redelegated to the Assistant Commandant for Marine Safety, Security and Environmental Protection, U.S. Coast Guard Headquarters, with the reservation that this authority shall not be further redelegated, the authority to grant exemptions from provisions of the Vessel Bridge-to-Bridge Radiotelephone Act and this part.

(b) Any person may petition for an exemption from any provision of the Act or this part;

(c) Each petition must be submitted in writing to Commandant (CG-DCO-D), Attn: Deputy for Operations Policy and Capabilities, U.S. Coast Guard Stop 7318, 2703 Martin Luther King Jr. Avenue, SE., Washington, DC 20593-7318, and must state:

(1) The provisions of the Act or this part from which an exemption is requested; and

(2) The reasons why marine navigation will not be adversely affected if the exemption is granted and if the exemption relates to a local communication system how that system would fully comply with the intent of the concept of the Act but would not conform in detail if the exemption is granted.

VESSEL BRIDGE-TO-BRIDGE
RADIOTELEPHONE—CONTINUED

§ 26.09 List of Exemptions.

(a) All vessels navigating on those waters governed by the navigation rules for the Great Lakes and their connecting and tributary waters (33 U.S.C. 241 et seq.) are exempt from the requirements of the Vessel Bridge-to-Bridge Radiotelephone Act and this part until May 6, 1975.

(b) Each vessel navigating on the Great Lakes as defined in the Inland Navigation Rules Act of 1980 (33 U.S.C. 2001 et seq.) and to which the Vessel Bridge-to-Bridge Radiotelephone Act (33 U.S.C. 1201-1208) applies is exempt from the requirements in 33 U.S.C. 1203, 1204, and 1205 and the regulations under §§ 26.03, 26.04, 26.05, 26.06, and 26.07. Each of these vessels and each person to whom 33 U.S.C. 1208(a) applies must comply with Articles VII, X, XI, XII, XIII, XV, and XVI and Technical Regulations 1-9 of "The Agreement Between the United States of America and Canada for Promotion of Safety on the Great Lakes by Means of Radio, 1973."

VESSEL TRAFFIC MANAGEMENT
33 CFR 161

Sec.

Subpart A – Vessel Traffic Services

GENERAL RULES

§ 161.1 Purpose and Intent.

(a) The purpose of this part is to promulgate regulations implementing and enforcing certain sections of the Ports and Waterways Safety Act (PWSA) setting up a national system of Vessel Traffic Services that will enhance navigation, vessel safety, and marine environmental protection, and promote safe vessel movement by reducing the potential for collisions, rammings, and groundings, and the loss of lives and property associated with these incidents within VTS areas established hereunder.

(b) Vessel Traffic Services provide the mariner with information related to the safe navigation of a waterway. This information, coupled with the mariner's compliance with the provisions set forth in this part, enhances the safe routing of vessels through congested waterways or waterways of particular hazard. Under certain circumstances, a VTS may issue directions to control the movement of vessels in order to minimize the risk of collision between vessels, or damage to property or the environment.

(c) The owner, operator, charterer, master, or person directing the movement of a vessel remains at all times responsible for the manner in which the vessel is operated and maneuvered, and is responsible for the safe navigation of the vessel under all circumstances. Compliance with these rules or with a direction of the VTS is at all times contingent upon the exigencies of safe navigation.

(d) Nothing in this part is intended to relieve any vessel, owner, operator, charterer, master, or person directing the movement of a vessel from the consequences of any neglect to comply with this part or any other applicable law or regulation (e.g., the International Regulations for Prevention of Collisions at Sea, 1972 (72 COLREGS) or the Inland Navigation Rules) or of the neglect of any precaution which may be required by the ordinary practice of seamen, or by the special circumstances of the case.

§ 161.2 Definitions.

For the purposes of this part:

Cooperative Vessel Traffic Services (CVTS) means the system of vessel traffic management established and jointly operated by the United States and Canada within adjoining waters. In addition, CVTS facilitates traffic movement and anchorages, avoids jurisdictional disputes, and renders assistance in emergencies in adjoining United States and Canadian waters.

Hazardous Vessel Operating Condition means any condition related to a vessel's ability to safely navigate or maneuver, and includes, but is not limited to:

(1) The absence or malfunction of vessel operating equipment, such as propulsion machinery, steering gear, radar system, gyrocompass, depth sounding device, automatic radar plotting aid (ARPA), radiotelephone, Automatic Identification System equipment, navigational lighting, sound signaling devices or similar equipment.

(2) Any condition on board the vessel likely to impair navigation, such as lack of current nautical charts and publications, personnel shortage, or similar condition.

(3) Vessel characteristics that affect or restrict maneuverability, such as cargo or tow arrangement, trim, loaded condition, underkeel or overhead clearance, speed capabilities, power availability, or similar characteristics, which may affect the positive control or safe handling of the vessel or the tow.

Navigable waters means all navigable waters of the United States including the territorial sea of the United States, extending to 12 nautical miles from United States baselines, as described in Presidential Proclamation No. 5928 of December 27, 1988.

Precautionary Area means a routing measure comprising an area within defined limits where vessels must navigate with particular caution and within which the direction of traffic may be recommended.

Towing Vessel means any commercial vessel engaged in towing another vessel astern, alongside, or by pushing ahead.

Vessel Movement Center (VMC) means the shore-based facility that operates the vessel tracking system for a Vessel Movement Reporting System (VMRS) area or sector within such an area. The VMC does not necessarily have the capability or qualified personnel to interact with marine traffic, nor does it necessarily respond to traffic situations developing in the area, as does a Vessel Traffic Service (VTS).

Vessel Movement Reporting System (VMRS) means a mandatory reporting system used to monitor and track vessel movements. This is accomplished by a vessel providing information under established procedures as set forth in this part in the areas defined in Table 161.12(c) (VTS and VMRS Centers, Call Signs/MMSI, Designated Frequencies, and Monitoring Areas).

Vessel Movement Reporting System (VMRS) User means a vessel, or an owner, operator, charterer, Master, or person directing the movement of a vessel that is required to participate in a VMRS.

Vessel Traffic Center (VTC) means the shore-based facility that operates the vessel traffic service for the Vessel Traffic Service area or sector within such an area.

Vessel Traffic Services (VTS) means a service implemented by the United States Coast Guard designed to improve the safety and efficiency of vessel traffic and to protect the environment. The VTS has the capability to interact with marine traffic and respond to traffic situations developing in the VTS area.

Vessel Traffic Service Area or *VTS Area* means the geographical area encompassing a specific VTS area of service. This area of service may be subdivided into sectors for the purpose of allocating responsibility to individual Vessel Traffic Centers or to identify different operating requirements.

NOTE: Although regulatory jurisdiction is limited to the navigable waters of the United States, certain vessels will be encouraged or may be required, as a condition of port entry, to report beyond this area to facilitate traffic management within the VTS area.

VTS Special Area means a waterway within a VTS area in which special operating requirements apply.

VTS User means a vessel, or an owner, operator, charterer, master, or person directing the movement of a vessel, that is:
(a) Subject to the Vessel Bridge-to-Bridge Radiotelephone Act; or
(b) Required to participate in a VMRS within a VTS area (VMRS User).

VTS User's Manual means the manual established and distributed by the VTS to provide the mariner with a description of the services offered and rules in force for that VTS. Additionally, the manual may include chartlets showing the area and sector boundaries, general navigational information about the area, and procedures, radio frequencies, reporting provisions and other information which may assist the mariner while in the VTS area.

§ 161.3 Applicability.

The provisions of this subpart shall apply to each VTS User and may also apply to any vessel while underway or at anchor on the navigable waters of the United States within a VTS area, to the extent the VTS considers necessary.

§ 161.4 Requirement to carry the rules.

Each VTS User shall carry on board and maintain for ready reference a copy of these rules.

NOTE: These rules are contained in the applicable U.S. Coast Pilot, the VTS User's Manual which may be obtained by contacting the appropriate VTS, and periodically published in the Local Notice to Mariners. The VTS User's Manual and the World VTS Guide, an International Maritime Organization (IMO) recognized publication, contain additional information which may assist the prudent mariner while in the appropriate VTS area.

§ 161.5 Deviations from the rules.

(a) Requests to deviate from any provision in this part, either for an extended period of time or if anticipated before the start of a transit, must be submitted in writing to the appropriate District Commander. Upon receipt of the written request, the District Commander may authorize a deviation if it is determined that such a deviation provides a level of safety equivalent to that provided by the required measure or is a maneuver considered necessary for safe navigation under the circumstances. An application for an authorized deviation must state the need and fully describe the proposed alternative to the required measure.

(b) Requests to deviate from any provision in this part due to circumstances that develop during a transit or immediately preceding a transit, may be made verbally to the appropriate VTS Director. Requests to deviate shall be made as far in advance as practicable. Upon receipt of the request, the VTS Director may authorize a deviation if it is determined that, based on vessel handling characteristics, traffic density, radar contacts, environmental conditions and other relevant information, such a deviation provides a level of safety equivalent to that provided by the required measure or is a maneuver considered necessary for safe navigation under the circumstances.

§ 161.6 Preemption.

The regulations in this part have preemptive impact over State laws or regulations on the same subject matter. The Coast Guard has determined, after considering the factors developed by the Supreme Court in U.S. v. Locke, 529 U.S. 89 (2000), that by enacting Chapter 25 of the Ports and Waterways Safety Act (33 U.S.C. 1221 et seq.), Congress intended that Coast Guard regulations preempt State laws or regulations regarding vessel traffic services in United States ports and waterways.

SERVICES, VTS MEASURES, AND OPERATING REQUIREMENTS

§ 161.10 Services.

To enhance navigation and vessel safety, and to protect the marine environment, a VTS may issue advisories, or respond to vessel requests for information, on reported conditions within the VTS area, such as:

(a) Hazardous conditions or circumstances;

(b) Vessel congestion;

(c) Traffic density;

(d) Environmental conditions;

(e) Aids to navigation status;

(f) Anticipated vessel encounters;

(g) Another vessel's name, type, position, hazardous vessel operating conditions, if applicable, and intended navigation movements, as reported;

(h) Temporary measures in effect;

(i) A description of local harbor operations and conditions, such as ferry routes, dredging, and so forth;

(j) Anchorage availability; or

(k) Other information or special circumstances

§ 161.11 VTS measures.

(a) A VTS may issue measures or directions to enhance navigation and vessel safety and to protect the marine environment, such as, but not limited to:

(1) Designating temporary reporting points and procedures;

(2) Imposing vessel operating requirements; or

(3) Establishing vessel traffic routing schemes.

(b) During conditions of vessel congestion, restricted visibility, adverse weather, or other hazardous circumstances, a VTS may control, supervise, or otherwise manage traffic, by specifying times of entry, movement, or departure to, from, or within a VTS area.

§ 161.12 Vessel operating requirements.

(a) Subject to the exigencies of safe navigation, a VTS User shall comply with all measures established or directions issued by a VTS.

(b) If, in a specific circumstance, a VTS User is unable to safely comply with a measure or direction issued by the VTS, the VTS User may deviate only to the extent necessary to avoid endangering persons, property or the environment. The deviation shall be reported to the VTS as soon as is practicable.

(c) When not exchanging voice communications, a VTS User must maintain a listening watch as required by § 26.04(e) of this chapter on the VTS frequency designated in Table 161.12(c) (VTS and VMRS Centers, Call Signs/MMSI, Designated Frequencies, and Monitoring Areas). In addition, the VTS User must respond promptly when hailed and communicate in the English language.

NOTE TO § 161.12(c): As stated in 47 CFR 80.148(b), a very high frequency watch on Channel 16 (156.800 MHz) is not required on vessels subject to the Vessel Bridge-to-Bridge Radiotelephone Act and participating in a Vessel Traffic Service (VTS) system when the watch is maintained on both the vessel bridge-to-bridge frequency and a designated VTS frequency.

(d) As soon as is practicable, a VTS User shall notify the VTS of any of the following:

(1) A marine casualty as defined in 46 CFR 4.05-1;

(2) Involvement in the ramming of a fixed or floating object;

(3) A pollution incident as defined in § 151.15 of this chapter;

(4) A defect or discrepancy in an aid to navigation;

(5) A hazardous condition as defined in § 160.204 of this chapter

(6) Improper operation of vessel equipment required by part 164 of this chapter;

(7) A situation involving hazardous materials for which a report is required by 49 CFR 176.48; and

(8) A hazardous vessel operating condition as defined in § 161.2.

§ 161.13 VTS Special Area operating requirements.

The following operating requirements apply within a VTS Special Area:

(a) A VTS User shall, if towing astern, do so with as short a hawser as safety and good seamanship permits.

(b) A VMRS User shall:

(1) Not enter or get underway in the area without prior approval of the VTS;

(2) Not enter a VTS Special Area if a hazardous vessel operating condition or circumstance exists;

(3) Not meet, cross, or overtake any other VMRS User in the area without prior approval of the VTS; and

(4) Before meeting, crossing, or overtaking any other VMRS User in the area, communicate on the designated vessel bridge-to-bridge radiotelephone frequency, intended navigation movements, and any other information necessary in order to make safe passing arrangements. This requirement does not relieve a vessel of any duty prescribed by the International Regulations for Prevention of Collisions at Sea, 1972 (72 COLREGS) or the Inland Navigation Rules.

Subpart B—Vessel Movement Reporting System

§ 161.15 Purpose and intent.

(a) A Vessel Movement Reporting System (VMRS) is a system used to monitor and track vessel movements within a VTS or VMRS area. This is accomplished by requiring that vessels provide information under established procedures as set forth in this part, or as directed by the Center.

(b) To avoid imposing an undue reporting burden or unduly congesting radiotelephone frequencies, reports shall be limited to information which is essential to achieve the objectives of the VMRS. These reports are consolidated into three reports (sailing plan, position, and final).

§ 161.16 Applicability.

Unless otherwise stated, the provisions of this subpart apply to the following vessels and VMRS Users:

(a) Every power-driven vessel of 40 meters (approximately 131 feet) or more in length, while navigating;

(b) Every towing vessel of 8 meters (approximately 26 feet) or more in length, while navigating; or

(c) Every vessel certificated to carry 50 or more passengers for hire, when engaged in trade.

§ 161.17 Definitions.

As used in this subpart:

Center means a Vessel Traffic Center or Vessel Movement Center.

Published means available in a widely-distributed and publicly available medium (e.g., VTS User's Manual, ferry schedule, Notice to Mariners).

§ 161.18 Reporting requirements.

(a) A Center may:

(1) Direct a vessel to provide any of the information set forth in Table 161.18(a) (IMO Standard Ship Reporting System);

(2) Establish other means of reporting for those vessels unable to report on the designated frequency; or

(3) Require reports from a vessel in sufficient time to allow advance vessel traffic planning.

(b) All reports required by this part shall be made as soon as is practicable on the frequency designated in Table 161.12(c) (VTS and VMRS Centers, Call Signs/MMSI, Designated Frequencies, and Monitoring Areas).

(c) When not exchanging communications, a VMRS User must maintain a listening watch as described in § 26.04(e) of this chapter on the frequency designated in Table 161.12(c) (VTS and VMRS Centers, Call Signs/MMSI, Designated Frequencies, and Monitoring Areas). In addition, the VMRS User must respond promptly when hailed and communicate in the English language.

NOTE: As stated in 47 CFR 80.148(b), a VHF watch on Channel 16 (156.800 MHz) is not required on vessels subject to the Vessel Bridge-to-Bridge Radiotelephone Act and participating in a Vessel Traffic Service (VTS) system when the watch is maintained on both the vessel bridge-to-bridge frequency and a designated VTS frequency.

TABLE 161.18(A)—THE IMO STANDARD SHIP REPORTING SYSTEM

A	ALPHA	Ship	Name, call sign or ship station identity, and flag.
B	BRAVO	Dates and time of event	A 6 digit group giving day of month (first two digits), hours and minutes (last four digits). If other than UTC state time zone used.
C	CHARLIE	Position	A 4 digit group giving latitude in degrees and minutes suffixed with N (north) or S (south) and a 5 digit group giving longitude in degrees and minutes suffixed with E (east) or W (west); or.
D	DELTA	Position	True bearing (first 3 digits) and distance (state distance) in nautical miles from a clearly identified landmark (state landmark).
E	ECHO	True course	A 3 digit group.
F	FOXTROT	Speed in knots and tenths of knots	A 3 digit group.
G	GOLF	Port of Departure	Name of last port of call.
H	HOTEL	Date, time and point of entry system	Entry time expressed as in (B) and into the entry position expressed as in (C) or (D).
I	INDIA	Destination and expected time of arrival	Name of port and date time group expressed as in (B).
J	JULIET	Pilot	State whether a deep sea or local pilot is on board.
K	KILO	Date, time and point of exit from system	Exit time expressed as in (B) and exit position expressed as in (C) or (D).
L	LIMA	Route information	Intended track.
M	MIKE	Radio	State in full names of communications stations/frequencies guarded.
N	NOVEMBER	Time of next report	Date time group expressed as in (B).
O	OSCAR	Maximum present static draught in meters	4 digit group giving meters and centimeters.
P	PAPA	Cargo on board	Cargo and brief details of any dangerous cargoes as well as harmful substances and gases that could endanger persons or the environment.
Q	QUEBEC	Defects, damage, deficiencies or limitations	Brief detail of defects, damage, deficiencies or other limitations.
R	ROMEO	Description of pollution or dangerous goods lost	Brief details of type of pollution (oil, chemicals, etc) or dangerous goods lost overboard; position expressed as in (C) or (D).
S	SIERRA	Weather conditions	Brief details of weather and sea conditions prevailing.
T	TANGO	Ship's representative and/or owner	Details of name and particulars of ship's representative and/or owner for provision of information.
U	UNIFORM	Ship size and type	Details of length, breadth, tonnage, and type, etc., as required.
V	VICTOR	Medical personnel	Doctor, physician's assistant, nurse, no medic.
W	WHISKEY	Total number of persons on board	State number.
X	XRAY	Miscellaneous	Any other information as appropriate. [i.e., a detailed description of a planned operation, which may include: its duration; effective area; any restrictions to navigation; notification procedures for approaching vessels; in addition, for a towing operation: configuration, length of the tow, available horsepower, etc.; for a dredge or floating plant: configuration of pipeline, mooring configuration, number of assist vessels, etc.].

(d) A vessel must report:

(1) Any significant deviation from its Sailing Plan, as defined in § 161.19, or from previously reported information; or

(2) Any intention to deviate from a VTS issued measure or vessel traffic routing system.

(e) When reports required by this part include time information, such information shall be given using the local time zone in effect and the 24-hour military clock system.

§ 161.19 Sailing Plan (SP).

Unless otherwise stated, at least 15 minutes before navigating a VTS area, a vessel must report the:

(a) Vessel name and type;

(b) Position;

(c) Destination and ETA;

(d) Intended route;

(e) Time and point of entry; and

(f) Certain dangerous cargo on board or in its tow, as defined in §160.204 of this subchapter.

§ 161.20 Position Report (PR).

A vessel must report its name and position:

(a) Upon point of entry into a VMRS area;

(b) At designated reporting points as set forth in subpart C; or

(c) When directed by the Center.

§ 161.21 Automated reporting.

(a) Unless otherwise directed, vessels equipped with an Automatic Identification System (AIS) are required to make continuous, all stations, AIS broadcasts, in lieu of voice Position Reports, to those Centers denoted in Table 161.12(c) of this part.

(b) Should an AIS become non-operational, while or prior to navigating a VMRS area, it should be restored to operating condition as soon as possible, and, until restored a vessel must:

(1) Notify the Center;

(2) Make voice radio Position Reports at designated reporting points as required by § 161.20(b) of this part; and

(3) Make any other reports as directed by the Center.

§ 161.22 Final Report (FR).

A vessel must report its name and position:

(a) On arrival at its destination; or

(b) When leaving a VTS area

§ 161.23 Reporting exemptions.

(a) Unless otherwise directed, the following vessels are exempted from providing Position and Final Reports due to the nature of their operation:

(1) Vessels on a published schedule and route;

(2) Vessels operating within an area of a radius of three nautical miles or less; or

(3) Vessels escorting another vessel or assisting another vessel in maneuvering procedures. (b) A vessel described in paragraph (a) of this section must:

(1) Provide a Sailing Plan at least 5 minutes but not more than 15 minutes before navigating within the VMRS area; and

(2) If it departs from its promulgated schedule by more than 15 minutes or changes its limited operating area, make the established VMRS reports, or report as directed.

Subpart C—Vessel Traffic Service and Vessel Movement Reporting System Areas and Reporting Points

NOTE: All geographic coordinates contained in part 161 (latitude and longitude) are expressed in North American Datum of 1983 (NAD 83).

§ 161.25 Vessel Traffic Service New York Area.

The area consists of the navigable waters of the Lower New York Harbor bounded on the east by a line drawn from Norton Point to Breezy Point; on the south by a line connecting the entrance buoys at the Ambrose Channel, Swash Channel, and Sandy Hook Channel to Sandy Hook Point; and on the southeast including the waters of Sandy Hook Bay south to a line drawn at latitude 40°25' N.; then west into waters of the Raritan Bay to the Raritan River Rail Road Bridge; and then north including the waters of the Arthur Kill and Newark Bay to the Lehigh Valley Draw Bridge at latitude 40°41.9' N.; and then east including the waters of the Kill Van Kull and Upper New York Bay north to a line drawn east-west from the Holland Tunnel Ventilator Shaft at latitude 40°43.7' N., longitude 74°01.6' W. in the Hudson River; and then continuing east including the waters of the East River to the Throgs Neck Bridge, excluding the Harlem River.

NOTE: Although mandatory participation in VTSNY is limited to the area within the navigable waters of the United States, VTSNY will provide services beyond those waters. Prospective users are encouraged to report beyond the area of required participation in order to facilitate advance vessel traffic management in the VTS area and to receive VTSNY advisories and/or assistance.

§ 161.30 Vessel Traffic Service Louisville.

The VTS area consists of the navigable waters of the Ohio River between McAlpine Locks (Mile 606.8) and Twelve Mile Island (Mile 593), only when the McAlpine upper pool gauge is at 13.0 feet or above.

§ 161.35 Vessel Traffic Service Houston/Galveston.

(a) The VTS area consists of the following major waterways and portions of connecting waterways: Galveston Bay Entrance Channel; Outer Bar Channel; Inner Bar Channel; Bolivar Roads Channel; Galveston Channel; Gulf ICW and Galveston-Freeport Cut-Off from Mile 346 to Mile 352; Texas City Channel; Texas City Turning Basin; Texas City Canal Channel; Texas City Canal Turning Basin; Houston Ship Channel; Bayport Channel; Bayport Turning Basin; Houston Turning Basin; and the following precautionary areas associated with these waterways.

(b) *Precautionary areas.*

TABLE 161.35(B)—VTS HOUSTON/GALVESTON PRECAUTIONARY AREAS

Precautionary area name	Radius (yds.)	Center point	
		Latitude	Longitude
Bolivar Roads	4000	29°20.9' N	94°47.0' W
Red Fish Bar	4000	29°29.8' N	94°51.9' W
Bayport Channel	4000	29°36.7' N	94°57.2' W
Morgans Point	2000	29°41.0' N	94°59.0' W
Upper San Jacinto Bay	1000	29°42.3' N	95°01.1' W
Baytown	1000	29°43.6' N	95°01.4' W
Lynchburg	1000	29°45.8' N	95°04.8' W
Carpenters Bayou	1000	29°45.3' N	95°05.6' W
Jacintoport	1000	29°44.8' N	95°06.0' W
Greens Bayou	1000	29°44.8' N	95°10.2' W
Hunting Bayou	1000	29°44.3' N	95°12.1' W
Sims Bayou	1000	29°43.2' N	95°14.4' W
Brady Island	1000	29°43.5' N	95°16.4' W
Buffalo Bayou	1000	29°45.0' N	95°17.3' W

Note: Each Precautionary Area encompasses a circular area of the radius denoted.

(c) *Reporting points.*

TABLE 161.35(C)—VTS HOUSTON/GALVESTON REPORTING POINTS

Designator	Geographic name	Geographic description	Latitude/longitude	Notes
1	Galveston Bay Entrance Channel	Galveston Bay Entrance CH Lighted Buoy (LB) "1C"	29°18.2' N; 94°37.6' W	
2	Galveston Bay Entrance Channel	Galveston Bay Entrance Channel LB 11 and 12	29°20.6' N; 94°44.6' W	
E	Bolivar Land Cut	Mile 349 Intracoastal Waterway (ICW)	29°22.5' N; 94°46.9' W	Tows entering HSC also report at HSC LB 25 & 26.
W	Pelican Cut	Mile 351 ICW	29°21.4' N; 94°48.5' W	Tows entering HSC also report at HSC LB 25 & 26.
G	Galveston Harbor	Galveston Channel Lt. 2	29°20.2' N; 94°46.6' W	Coast Guard Base.
T	Texas City Channel	Texas City Channel Lt. 12	29°22.4' N; 94°50.9' W	
X	Houston Ship Channel ICW Intersection	Houston Ship Channel (HSC) LB 25 and 26	29°22.2' N; 94°48.1' W	Tow entering HSC from ICW or Texas Cut Only.
3	Lower Galveston Bay	HSC Lt. 31 and LB 32	29°23.8' N; 94°48.9' W	
4	Red Fish Bar	HSC Lt. 53 & 54	29°30.3' N; 94°52.4' W	
P	Bayport Ship Channel	Bayport Ship Channel Lt. 8 and 9	29°36.8' N; 94°59.5' W	Bayport Land Cut.
4A	Upper Galveston Bay	HSC Lt. 69 and 70	29°34.7' N; 94°55.8' W	Tows only.
5	Morgan's Point	HSC Lt. 91	29°41.0' N; 94°59.0' W	
6	Exxon	HSC Lt. 109A	29°43.5' N; 95°01.4' W	
7	Lynchburg	Ferry crossing	29°45.8' N; 95°04.8' W	
8	Shell Oil	Boggy Bayou	29°44.1' N; 95°08.0' W	
9	Greens Bayou	HSC Lt. 152	29°44.8' N; 95°10.1' W	
10	Hunting Bayou	Hunting Bayou Turning Basin.	29°44.4' N; 95°12.1' W	
11	Lyondell	Sims Bayou Turning Basin.	29°43.2' N; 95°14.4' W	
12	I-610 Bridge	I-610 Bridge	29°43.5' N; 95°16.0' W	
13	Buffalo Bayou	Houston Turning Basin	29°45.0' N; 95°17.4' W	

§ 161.40 Vessel Traffic Service Berwick Bay.

(a) The VTS area consists of the navigable waters of the following segments of waterways: the Intracoastal Waterway (ICW) Morgan City to Port Allen Alternate Route from Mile Marker 0 to Mile Marker 5; the ICW from Mile Marker 93 west of Harvey Lock (WHL) to Mile Marker 102 WHL; the Atchafalaya River Route from Mile Marker 113 to Mile Marker 122; from Bayou Shaffer Junction (ICW Mile Marker 94.5 WHL) south one statute mile along Bayou Shaffer; and from Berwick Lock northwest one statute mile along the Lower Atchafalaya River.

(b) VTS Special Area. The Berwick Bay VTS Special Area consists of those waters within a 1000 yard radius of the Burlington Northern/Santa Fe Railroad Bridge located at Mile .03 MC/PA.

(c) Reporting Points.

TABLE 161.40(C)—VTS BERWICK BAY REPORTING POINTS

Designator	Geographic name	Geographic description	Latitude/longitude	Notes
1	Stouts Pass	Stouts Point Light "1" Mile 113-Atchafalaya River	29°43'47" N 91°13'25" W	
2	Berwick Lock	Mile 1.9 MC/PA	29°43'10" N 91°13'28" W	If transiting the Lock.
3	Conrad's Point Junction	Buoy "1" Mile 1.5 MC/PA	29°42'32" N 91°13'14" W	
4	Swift Ships Flat Lake Junction	Mile 3 MC/PA	29°43'26" N 91°12'22" W	
5	Burlington Northern/Santa Fe Railroad Bridge	Mile 0.3 MC/PA	29°41'34" N 91°12'44" W	
6	20 Grant Point Junction	Bayou Boeuf-Atchafalaya R. Mile 95.5 ICW	29°41'18" N 91°12'36" W	
7	ICW	Overhead Power Cable Mile 96.5 ICW	29°40'43" N 91°13'18" W	
8	Wax Bayou Junction	Light "A" Mile 98.2W ICW	29°39'29" N 91°14'46" W	
9	Shaffer Junction	ICW-Bayou Shaffer Mile 94.5 ICW	29°41'10" N 91°11'38" W	

§ 161.45 Vessel Traffic Service St. Marys River.

(a) The VTS area consists of the navigable waters of the St. Marys River and lower Whitefish Bay from 45°57' N. (De Tour Reef Light) to the south, to 46°38.7' N. (Ile Parisienne Light) to the north, except the waters of the St. Marys Falls Canal, and to the east along a line from La Pointe to Sims Point, within Potagannissing Bay and Worsley Bay.

(b) Reporting Points.

TABLE 161.45(B)—VTS ST. MARYS RIVER REPORTING POINTS

Designator	Geographic name	Geographic description	Latitude/longitude	Notes
1	Ile Parisienne	Ile Parisienne Light	46°37.3' N; 84°45.9' W	Downbound Only.
2	Gros Cap Reef	Gros Cap Reefs Light	46°30.6' N; 84°37.1' W	Upbound Only.
3	Round Island	Round Island Light 32	46°26.9' N; 84°31.7'W.	
4	Pointe Louise	Pointe Louise Light	46°27.8' N; 84°28.2'W.	
5*	West End of Locks	West Center Pierhead Light	46°30.2' N; 84°22.2' W	Upbound Only.
6	East End of Locks	East Center Pierhead Light	46°30.1' N; 84°20.3' W	Downbound Only.
7	Mission Point	Light 99	46°29.2' N; 84°18.1'W.	
8	Six Mile Point	Six Mile Point	46°26.1' N; 84°15.4'W.	
9	Ninemile Point	Light 80	46°23.5' N; 84°14.1'W.	
10	West Neebish Channel	Light 29	46°16.9' N; 84°12.5' W	Downbound Only.
11	Munuscong Lake Junction	Lighted Junction Buoy	46°10.8' N; 84°05.6'W.	
12	De Tour Reef	De Tour Reef Light	46°56.9' N; 83°53.7' W.	

§ 161.50 Vessel Traffic Service San Francisco.

The VTS area consists of all the navigable waters of San Francisco Bay Region south of the Mare Island Causeway Bridge and the Petaluma River Entrance Channel Daybeacon 19 and Petaluma River Entrance Channel Light 20 and north of the Dumbarton Bridge; its seaward approaches within a 38 nautical mile radius of Mount Tamalpais (37-55.8' N., 122-34.6' W.); and its navigable tributaries as far east as the port of Stockton on the San Joaquin River, as far north as the port of Sacramento on the Sacramento River.

§ 161.55 Vessel Traffic Service Puget Sound and the Cooperative Vessel Traffic Service for the Juan de Fuca Region.

The Vessel Traffic Service Puget Sound area consists of the navigable waters of the United States bounded by a line drawn from the Washington State coastline at 48°23′08″ N., 124°43′37″ W. on Cape Flattery to the Cape Flattery Light at 48°23′30″ N., 124°44′12″ W. on Tatoosh Island, due west to the U.S. Territorial Sea Boundary; thence northward along the U.S. Territorial Sea Boundary to its intersection with the U.S./Canada International Boundary; thence east along the U.S./Canada International Boundary through the waters known as the Strait of Juan de Fuca, Haro Strait, Boundary Pass, and the Strait of Georgia to the Washington State coastline at 49°00′06″ N., 122°45′18″ W. (International Boundary Range C Rear Light). This area includes: Puget Sound, Hood Canal, Possession Sound, the San Juan Island Archipelago, Rosario Strait, Guemes Channel, Bellingham Bay, the U.S. waters of the Strait of Juan de Fuca and the Strait of Georgia, and all waters adjacent to the above.

(a) Vessel Traffic Service Puget Sound participates in a U.S./Canadian Cooperative Vessel Traffic Service (CVTS) to jointly manage vessel traffic in the Juan de Fuca Region. The CVTS for the Juan de Fuca Region consists of all waters of the Strait of Juan de Fuca and its offshore approaches, southern Georgia Strait, the Gulf and San Juan Archipelagos, Rosario Strait, Boundary Pass and Haro Strait, bounded on the northwest by 48°35′45″ N.; and on the southwest by 48°23′30″ N.; and on the west by the rhumb line joining 48°35′45″ N., 124°47′30″ W. with 48°23′30″ N., 124°48′37″ W.; and on the northeast in the Strait of Georgia, by a line drawn along 49° N. from Vancouver Island to Semiahmoo Bay; and on the southeast, by a line drawn from McCurdy Point on the Quimper Peninsula to Point Partridge on Whidbey Island. Canadian and United States Vessel Traffic Centers (Tofino, B.C., Canada, Vancouver, BC, Canada and Seattle, WA) manage traffic within the CVTS area irrespective of the International Boundary.

(b) VTS Special Area: The Eastern San Juan Island Archipelago VTS Special Area consists of all waters of the eastern San Juan Island Archipelago including: Rosario Strait bounded to the south by latitude 48°26.40′ N. (the center of the Precautionary Area "RB") extending from Lopez Island to Fidalgo Island, and to the north by latitude 48°40.57′ N. (the center of the Precautionary Area "C") extending from Orcas Island to Lummi Island; Guemes Channel; Bellingham Channel; Padilla Bay and southern Bellingham Bay (Samish Bay) south of latitude 48°38.42′N.

NOTE: The center of precautionary area "RB" is not marked by a buoy. All precautionary areas are depicted on National Oceanic and Atmospheric Administration (NOAA) nautical charts.

(c) Additional VTS Special Area Operating Requirements. The following additional requirements are applicable in the Eastern San Juan Island Archipelago VTS Special Area:

(1) A vessel engaged in towing shall not impede the passage of a vessel of 40,000 dead weight tons or more.

(2) A vessel of less than 40,000 dead weight tons is exempt from the provision set forth in §161.13(b)(1) of this part.

(3) A vessel of less than 100 meters in length is exempt from the provisions set forth in §161.13(b)(3) of this part.

(4) Approval will not be granted for:

(i) A vessel of 100 meters or more in length to meet or overtake a vessel of 40,000 dead weight tons or more;

(ii) A vessel of 40,000 dead weight tons or more to meet or overtake a vessel of 100 meters or more in length;

(iii) A vessel of 100 meters or more in length to cross or operate within 2,000 yards (except when crossing astern) of a vessel of 40,000 deadweight tons or more; or

(iv) A vessel of 40,000 dead weight tons or more to or cross or operate within 2,000 yards (except when crossing astern) of a vessel of 100 meters or more in length.

(d) Reporting Point. Inbound vessels in the Strait of Juan de Fuca upon crossing 124-W.

§161.60 Vessel Traffic Service Prince William Sound.

(a) The VTS area consists of the navigable waters of the United States north of a line drawn from Cape Hinchinbrook Light to Schooner Rock Light, comprising that portion of Prince William Sound between 146°30' W. and 147°20' W. and includes Valdez Arm, Valdez Narrows and Port Valdez.

(b) The Valdez Arm VTS Special Area consists of the waters of the Valdez Arm Traffic Separation Scheme (described in § 167.1703 of this chapter); the waters northeast of a line drawn from shoreline to shoreline through the points 60°58.04' N, 146°46.52' W and 60°58.93' N, 146°48.86' W; and southwest of a line bearing 307° True from Tongue Point at 61°02.10' N, 146°40.00' W.

(c) The Valdez Narrows VTS Special Area consists of those waters of Valdez Arm, Valdez Narrows, and Port Valdez northeast of a line bearing 307° True from Tongue Point at 61°02'06"N., 146°40' W.; and southwest of a line bearing 307° True from Entrance Island Light at 61°05'06" N., 146°36'42" W.

(d) Additional VTS Special Area Operating Requirements. The following additional requirements are applicable in the Valdez Narrows VTS Special Area:

(1) No VMRS User shall proceed north of 61° N. without prior approval of the VTS.

(2) For a vessel listed in paragraph (c)(3) of this section—

(i) Approval to enter this area will not be granted to a vessel when a tank vessel of more than 20,000 deadweight tons is navigating therein;

(ii) A northbound vessel shall remain south of 61° N. until the VTS has granted permission to proceed; and

(iii) A southbound vessel shall remain in Port Valdez east of 146°35' W. and north of 61°06' N. until the VTS has granted permission to proceed.

(3) Paragraph (c)(2) of this section applies to—

(i) A vessel of 1600 gross tons or more; and

(ii) A towing vessel of 8 meters or more in length, except for a vessel performing duties as an escort vessel as defined in 33 CFR Part 168.

(e) Reporting Points.

TABLE 161.60(D)—VTS PRINCE WILLIAM SOUND REPORTING POINTS

Designator	Geographic name	Geographic description	Latitude/longitude	Notes
1A	Cape Hinchinbrook	Cape Hinchinbrook	60°16'18" N; 146°45'30" W	Northbound Only.
1B	Schooner Rock	Schooner Rock	60°18'42" N; 146°51'36" W	Southbound Only.
2A	Naked Island	Naked Island	60°40'00" N; 147°01'24" W	Northbound Only.
2B	Naked Island	Naked Island	60°40'00" N; 147°05'00" W	Southbound Only.
3A	Bligh Reef	Bligh Reef Light (Pilot Embark)	60°50'36" N; 146°57'30" W	Northbound Only.
3B	Bligh Reef	Bligh Reef Light (Pilot Disembark)	60°51'00" N; 147°01'24" W	Southbound Only.
4A	Rocky Point	Rocky Point	60°57'48" N; 146°47'30" W	Northbound Only.
4B	Rocky Point	Rocky Point	60°57'48" N; 146°50'00" W	Southbound Only.
5	Entrance Island	Entrance Island Light	61°05'24" N; 146°37'30" W.	

§ 161.65 Vessel Traffic Service Lower Mississippi River.

(a) The Vessel Traffic Service (VTS) area consists of navigable waters of the Lower Mississippi River (LMR) below 30°38.7' N 91°17.5' W (Port Hudson Light at 254.5 miles Above Head of Passes (AHP)), the Southwest Pass, and those within a 12-nautical mile radius around 28°54.3' N 89°25.7' W (Southwest Pass Entrance Light at 20.1 miles Below Head of Passes).

(b) The Algiers Point VTS Special Area consists of the navigable waters of the LMR bounded on the north by a line drawn from 29°57.62' N 90°02.61' W to 29°57.34' N 90°02.60' W and on the south by a line drawn from 29°56.89' N 90°03.72' W to 29°56.93' N 90°03.34' W (95.0 and 93.5 miles AHP) during periods of high water—that is, when the Carrolton Gage reads 8.0 feet or above on a rising stage or 9.0 feet or above on a falling stage, or under any other water conditions the Captain of the Port (COTP) deems necessary.

(c) *Additional Algiers Point VTS Special Area Operating Requirements.* The following additional requirements are applicable in the Algiers Point VTS Special Area:

(1) A vessel movement reporting system (VMRS) user must abide by the signals of the Governor Nicholls Street Wharf, 29°57.6' N 90°03.4' W, and Gretna, 29°55.5' N 90°03.7' W, Control Lights (94.3 and 96.6 miles AHP, respectively) in the following manner:

(i) *Green Light*—May proceed as intended.

(ii) *Red Light*—Do not proceed, unless otherwise directed by the VTS.

(iii) *No Light*—Do not proceed, immediately notify VTS and await further directions.

NOTE TO § 161.65(c)(1): To provide advance notification to downbound vessels, a traffic repeater signal of Gretna Light is located at Westwego, LA, 29°54.8' N; 90°08.3' W (101.4 miles AHP).

(2) A vessel awaiting a signal change or VTS directions must keep clear of other vessels transiting the area.

(d) The Eighty-one Mile Point VTS Special Area consists of navigable waters of the LMR between 167.5 miles AHP and 187.9 miles AHP.

(e) *Additional Eighty-one Mile Point VTS Special Area Operating Requirements.* The following additional requirements are applicable in the Eighty-one Mile Point VTS Special Area:

(1) Prior to proceeding upriver past 167.5 miles AHP, Sunshine Bridge, vessels must contact VTS New Orleans on VHF Channel 5A to check-in. Vessels must provide name and destination, confirm proper operation of their automated identification system (AIS) if required under 33 CFR 164.46, and, if applicable, size of tow and number of loaded and empty barges. At 173.7 miles AHP, Bringier Point Light, ascending vessels must contact VTS New Orleans and provide a follow-on position check. At both check-in and follow-on position check, VTS New Orleans will advise the vessel on traffic approaching Eighty-one Mile Point.

(2) Prior to proceeding downriver past 187.9 miles AHP COS-MAR Lights, vessels must contact VTS New Orleans on VHF Channel 5A to check-in. Vessels must provide name and destination, confirm proper operation of their AIS if required under 33 CFR 164.46, and, if applicable, size of tow and number of loaded and empty barges. At 183.9 miles AHP, Wyandotte Chemical Dock Lights, descending vessels must contact VTS New Orleans and provide a follow-on position check. At both check-in and follow-on position check, VTS New Orleans will advise the vessel on traffic approaching Eighty-one Mile Point.

(3) All vessels getting underway between miles 167.5 and 187.9 AHP must check-in with VTS New Orleans on VHF Channel 5A immediately prior to getting underway and must comply with the respective ascending and descending check-in and follow-on points listed in paragraphs (e)(1) and (2) of this section.

(4) Fleet vessels must checkin with VTS New Orleans if they leave their respective fleet or if they move into the main channel. Fleet vessels are not required to checkin if they are operating exclusively within their fleet.

(f) *Reporting Points.* Table 161.65(f) lists the VTS Lower Mississippi River Reporting Points.

TABLE 161.65(F)—VTS LOWER MISSISSIPPI RIVER REPORTING POINTS

Designator	Geographic name	Geographic description	Latitude/longitude/mile marker	Notes
A	Algiers Canal Forebay	88.0 AHP	29°55.40' N; 89°57.7' W	Upbound transiting Algiers Point Special Area.
B	Industrial Canal	92.7 AHP	29°57.2' N; 90°01.68' W	Upbound transiting Algiers Point Special Area.
C	Crescent Towing Smith Fleet	93.5 AHP	29°57.50' N; 90°02.62' W	Upbound Towing vessels transiting Algiers Point Special Area.
D	Marlex Terminal (Naval Ships)	99.0 AHP	29°54.65' N; 90°05.87' W	Downbound transiting Algiers Point Special Area.
E	Huey P Long Bridge	106.1 AHP	29°56.6' N; 90°10.1' W	Downbound transiting Algiers Point Special Area.

183

§ 161.70 Vessel Traffic Service Port Arthur.

(a) The VTS area consists of the navigable waters of the United States to the limits of the territorial seas bound by the following points: 30°10.00′ N., 92°37.00′ W.; then south to 29°10.00′ N., 92°37.00′ W.; then west to 29°10.00′ N., 93°52.25′ W.; then northwest to 29°33.70′ N., 94°21.25′ W.; then north to 30°10.00′ N., 94°21.25′ W.; then east along the 30°10′ N. latitude to the origination point.

NOTE: Although mandatory participation in VTS Port Arthur is limited to the area within the navigable waters of the United States, prospective users are encouraged to report at the safe water marks in order to facilitate vessel traffic management in the VTS Area and to receive advisories or navigational assistance.

(b) Precautionary areas.

TABLE 161.70(B)—VTS PORT ARTHUR PRECAUTIONARY AREAS

Precautionary area name	Radius	Center point latitude	Center point longitude
Petco Bend[1]	2000 yds	30°00.80′ N.	93°57.60′ W.
Black Bayou[1]	2000 yds	30°00.00′ N.	93°46.20′ W.
Orange Cut[1]	2000 yds	30°03.25′ N.	93°43.20′ W.
Neches River Intersection[1]	2000 yds	29°58.10′ N.	93°51.25′ W.
Texaco Island Intersection[1]	2000 yds	29°49.40′ N.	94°57.55′ W.
Sabine-Neches Waterway	N/A	All waters of the Sabine-Neches Waterway between the Texaco Island Precautionary Area and the Humble Island Precautionary Area.	

[1] Precautionary Area encompasses a circular area of the radius denoted around the center point with the exception of the Sabine-Neches Waterway.

(c) Reporting points (Inbound).

TABLE 161.70(C)—INBOUND

Designator	Geographic name	Geographic description	Latitude/ longitude	Notes
1	Sabine Bank Channel "SB" Buoy	Sabine Bank Sea Buoy	29°25.00′ N. 93°40.00′ W.	Sailing Plan Report
2	Sabine Pass Buoys "29/30"	Sabine Pass Buoys "29/30"	29°35.90′ N. 93°48.20′ W.	
3	Port Arthur Canal Light "43"	Keith Lake	29°46.50′ N. 93°56.47′ W.	
4	North Forty GIWW Mile 279	North Forty	29°56.40′ N. 93°52.10′ W.	
5	FINA Highline Neches River Light "19"	FINA Highline	29°59.10′ N. 93°54.30′ W.	
6	Ready Reserve Fleet Highline	Channel at Cove Mid-Point	30°00.80′ N. 93°59.90′ W.	
7	Sabine River MM 268	268 Highline	30°02.20′ N. 93°44.30′ W.	

(d) Reporting points (Outbound).

TABLE 161.70(D)—OUTBOUND

Designator	Geographic name	Geographic description	Latitude/ longitude	Notes
1	Sabine River Light "2"	Black Bayou	30°00.00' N. 93°46.25' W.	
2	Ready Reserve Fleet Highline	Channel at Cove Mid-Point	30°00.80' N. 93°59.90' W.	
3	FINA Highline Neches River Light "19"	FINA Highline	29°59.09' N. 93°54.30' W.	
4	GIWW Mile 285	The School House	29°52.70' N. 93°55.55' W.	*Sector Shift*
5	Port Arthur Canal Light "43"	Keith Lake	29°46.50' N. 93°56.47' W.	
6	Sabine Pass Buoys "29/30"	Sabine Pass Buoys "29/30"	29°35.90' N. 93°48.20' W.	
7	Sabine Bank Channel "SB" Buoy	Sabine Bank Sea Buoy	29°25.00' N. 93°40.00' W.	Final Report

(e) Reporting points (Eastbound).

TABLE 161.70(E)—EASTBOUND (ICW)

Designator	Geographic name	Geographic description	Latitude/ longitude	Notes
1	GIWW Mile 295	ICW MM 295	29°47.25' N. 94°01.10' W.	Sailing Plan Report.
2	North Forty GIWW Mile 279	North Forty	29°56.40' N. 93°52.10' W.	
3	Sabine River MM 268	268 Highline	30°02.20' N. 93°44.30' W.	
4	GIWW Mile 260	260 Highline	30°03.50' N. 93°37.50' W.	Final Report.

(f) Reporting points (Westbound).

TABLE 161.70(F)—WESTBOUND (ICW)

Designator	Geographic name	Geographic description	Latitude/ longitude	Notes
1	GIWW Mile 260	260 Highline	30°03.50' N. 93°37.50' W.	Sailing Plan Report.
2	Sabine River Light "2"	Black Bayou	30°00.03' N. 93°46.18' W.	
3	GIWW Mile 285	The School House	29°52.71' N. 93°55.55' W.	Sector Shift.
4	GIWW Mile 295	ICW MM 295	29°46.20' N. 94°02.60' W.	Final Report.

(g) Reporting points (Offshore Safety Fairway).

TABLE 161.70(G)—OFFSHORE SAFETY FAIRWAY

Designator	Geographic name	Geographic description	Latitude/ longitude	Notes
1	Sabine Pass Safety Fairway—East	East Dogleg	29°35.00' N. 93°28.00' W.	
2	Sabine Pass Safety Fairway—West	West Dogleg	29°28.00' N. 93°58.00' W.	

Table 161.12(c) – VTS and VMRS Centers, Call Signs/MMSI, Designated Frequencies, and Monitoring

(a)

Center —MMSI[1] Call Sign	Designated frequency (Channel Designation) —purpose[2]	Monitoring area[3,4]
Berwick Bay —03669950 Berwick Traffic	156.550 MHz (Ch. 11)	The waters south of 29°45' N., west of 91°10' W., north of 29°37' N., and east of 91°18' W.
Buzzards Bay Buzzards Bay Control[5]	156.600 MHz (Ch. 12)	The waters east and north of a line drawn from the southern tangent of Sakonnet Point, Rhode Island, in approximate position latitude 41°27.20' N., longitude 71°11.70' W., to the Buzzards Bay Entrance Light in approximate position latitude 41°23.8' N., longitude 71°02.00' W., and then to the southwestern tangent of Cuttyhunk Island, Massachusetts, at approximate position latitude 41°24.60' N., longitude 70°57.00' W., and including all of the Cape Cod Canal to its eastern entrance, except that the area of New Bedford harbor within the confines (north of) the hurricane barrier, and the passages through the Elizabeth Islands, is not considered to be "Buzzards Bay".
Houston-Galveston —003669954 Houston Traffic	156.550 MHz (Ch. 11) 156.250 MHz (Ch. 5A) —For Sailing Plans only	The navigable waters north of 29° N., west of 94°20' W., south of 29°49' N., and east of 95°20' W. The navigable waters north of a line extending due west from the southern most end of Exxon Dock #1 (20°43.37' N., 95°01.27' W.).
Houston Traffic	156.600 MHz (Ch. 12) 156.250 MHz (Ch. 5A) —For Sailing Plans only	The navigable waters south of a line extending due west from the southern most end of Exxon Dock #1 (29°43.37' N., 95°01.27' W.)
Los Angeles/Long Beach San Pedro Traffic	156.700 MHz (Ch.14)	*Vessel Movement Reporting System Area:* The navigable waters within a 25 nautical mile radius of Point Fermin Light (33°42.3' N., 118°17.6' W.).
Louisville Louisville Traffic	156.650 MHz (Ch. 13)	The waters of the Ohio River between McAlpine Locks (Mile 606) and Twelve Mile Island (Mile 593), only when the McAlpine upper pool gauge is at approximately 13.0 feet or above.
Lower Mississippi River[6] —0036699952 New Orleans Traffic	156.700 MHz (Ch.11)	The navigable waters of the Lower Mississippi River below 29°55.3' N 089°55.6' W (Saxonholm Light) at 86.0 miles Above Head of Passes (AHP), extending down river to Southwest Pass, and, within a 12 nautical mile radius around 28°54.3' N 089°25.7' W (Southwest Pass Entrance Light at 20.1 miles Below Head of Passes.
New Orleans Traffic	156.600 MHz (Ch.12)	The navigable waters of the Lower Mississippi River bounded on the north by a line drawn perpendicular on the river at 29°55'30" N 090°12'46" W (Upper Twelve Mile Point) at 109.0 miles AHP and on the south by a line drawn perpendicularly at 29°55.3' N 089°55.6' W (Saxonholm Light) at 86.0 miles AHP.
New Orleans Traffic	156.600 MHz (Ch.05A)	The navigable waters of the Lower Mississippi River below 30°38.7' N 091°17.5' W (Port Hudson Light) at 254.5 miles AHP bounded on the south by a line drawn perpendicular on the river at 29°55'30" N and 090°12'46" W (Upper Twelve Mile Point) at 109.0 miles AHP.

Table 161.12(c) – VTS and VMRS Centers, Call Signs/MMSI, Designated Frequencies, and Monitoring

Center –MMSI[1] Call Sign	Designated frequency (Channel Designation) –purpose[2]	Monitoring area[3,4]
New York —003669951		
New York Traffic	156.550 MHz (Ch. 11) —For Sailing Plans only; 156.600 MHz (Ch. 12) —For vessels at anchor	The area consists of the navigable waters of the Lower New York Bay bounded on the east by a line drawn from Norton Point to Breezy Point; on the south by a line connecting the entrance buoys at the Ambrose Channel, Swash Channel, and Sandy Hook Channel, and Sandy Hook Point; and on the southeast including the waters of Sandy Hook Bay south to a line drawn at latitude 40°25' N; then west in the Raritan Bay to the Raritan River Railroad Bridge, then north into waters of the Arthur Kill and Newark Bay to the Lehigh Valley Draw Bridge at latitude 40°41.9' N; and then east including the waters of the Kill Van Kull and the Upper New York Bay north to a line drawn east-west from the Holland Tunnel ventilator shaft at latitude 40°43.7' N, longitude 74°01.6' W, in the Hudson River; and then continuing east including the waters of the East River to the Throgs Neck Bridge, excluding the Harlem River.
New York Traffic	156.700 MHz (Ch. 14)	The navigable waters of the Lower New York Bay west of a line drawn from Norton Point to Breezy Point; and north of a line connecting the entrance buoys of Ambrose Channel, Swash Channel, and Sandy Hook Channel, to Sandy Hook Point; on the southeast including the waters of the Sandy Hook Bay south to a line drawn at latitude 40°25' N; then west into the waters of Raritan Bay East Reach to a line drawn from Great Kills Light south through Raritan Bay East Reach LGB #14 to Comfort PT, NJ; then north including the waters of the Upper New York Bay south of 40°42.40' N (Brooklyn Bridge) and 40°43.70' N (Holland Tunnel Ventilator Shaft); west through the KVK into the waters of the Arthur Kill north of 40°38.25' N (Arthur Kill Railroad Bridge); then north into the waters of the Newark Bay, south of 40°41.95' N (Lehigh Valley Draw Bridge).
New York Traffic	156.600 MHz (Ch. 12)	The navigable waters of the Raritan Bay south to a line drawn at latitude 40°26' N; then west of a line drawn from Great Kills Light south through the Raritan Bay East Reach LGB #14 to Point Comfort, NJ; then west to the Raritan River Railroad Bridge; and north including the waters of the Arthur Kill to 40°28.25' N (Arthur Kill Railroad Bridge); including the waters of the East River north of 40°42.40' N (Brooklyn Bridge) to the Throgs Neck Bridge, excluding the Harlem River.
Port Arthur —003669955		
Port Arthur Traffic	156.050 MHz (Ch. 01A)	*The navigable waters of the Sabine-Neches Canal south of 29°52.70' N.; Port Arthur Canal; Sabine Pass Channel; Sabine Bank Channel; Sabine Outer Bar Channel; the offshore safety fairway; and the ICW from High Island to its intersection with the Sabine-Neches Canal.*
Port Arthur Traffic	156.275 MHz (Ch. 65A)	*The navigable waters of the Neches River, Sabine River, and Sabine-Neches Waterway north of 29°52.70' N.; and the ICW from its intersection with the Sabine River to MM 260.*
Port Arthur Traffic	156.675 MHz (Ch 73)[6]	*The navigable waters of the Calcasieu Channel; Calcasieu River Channel; and the ICW from MM 260 to MM 191.*
Prince William Sound — 003669958		
Valdez Traffic[7]	156.650 MHz (Ch. 13)	The navigable waters south of 61°05' N, east of 147°20' W., north of 60° N., and west of 146°30' W.; and, all navigable waters in Port Valdez.
Puget Sound[7]		
Seattle Traffic —003669957	156.700 MHz (Ch. 14)	The waters of Puget Sound, Hood Canal and adjacent waters south of a line connecting Nodule Point and Bush Point in Admiralty Inlet and south of a line drawn due east from the southernmost tip of Possession Point on Whidbey Island to the shoreline.
Seattle Traffic —003669957	156.250 MHz (Ch. 5A)	The waters of the Strait of Juan de Fuca east of 124°40' W., excluding the waters in the central portion of the Strait of Juan de Fuca north and east of Race Rocks; the navigable waters of the Strait of Georgia east of 122°52' W.; the San Juan Island Archipelago, Rosario Strait, Bellingham Bay; Admiralty Inlet north of a line connecting Nodule Point and Bush Point and all waters east of Whidbey Island North of a line drawn due east from the southernmost tip of Possession Point on Whidbey Island to the shoreline.
Tofino Traffic —003160012	156.725 MHz (Ch. 74)	The waters west of 124°40' W. within 50 nautical miles of the coast of Vancouver Island including the waters north of 48° N., and east of 127° W.
Victoria Traffic —03160010	156.550 MHz (Ch. 11)	The waters of the Strait of Georgia west of 122°52' W., the navigable waters of the central Strait of Juan de Fuca north and east of Race Rocks, including the Gulf Island Archipelago, Boundary Pass and Haro Strait.

Table 161.12(c) – VTS and VMRS Centers, Call Signs/MMSI, Designated Frequencies, and Monitoring

Center —MMSI[1] Call Sign	Designated frequency (Channel Designation) —purpose[2]	Monitoring area[3,4]
San Francisco —003669956		
San Francisco Traffic	156.700 MHz (Ch. 14)	The navigable waters of the San Francisco Offshore Precautionary Area, the navigable waters shoreward of the San Francisco Offshore Precautionary Area east of 122°42.0′ W. and north of 37°40.0′ N. extending eastward through the Golden Gate, and the navigable waters of San Francisco Bay and as far east as the port of Stockton on the San Joaquin River, as far north as the port of Sacramento on the Sacramento River.
San Francisco Traffic	156.600 MHz (Ch. 12)	The navigable waters within a 38 nautical mile radius of Mount Tamalpais (37°55.8′ N., 122°34.6′ W.) west of 122°42.0′ W. and south of 37°40.0′ N and excluding the San Francisco Offshore Precautionary Area.
St. Marys River —003669953		
Soo Traffic	156.600 MHz (Ch. 12)	The waters of the St. Marys River between 45°57′ N. (De Tour Reef Light) and 46°38.7′ N. (Ile Parisienne Light), except the St. Marys Falls Canal and those navigable waters east of a line from 46°04.16′ N. and 46°01.57′ N. (La Pointe to Sims Point in Potagannissing Bay and Worsley Bay).

Notes:

[1] Maritime Mobile Service Identifier (MMSI) is a unique nine-digit number assigned that identifies ship stations, ship earth stations, coast stations, coast earth stations, and group calls for use by a digital selective calling (DSC) radio, an INMARSAT ship earth station or AIS. AIS requirements are set forth in §§161.21 and 164.46 of this subchapter. The requirements set forth in §§161.21 and 164.46 of this subchapter apply in those areas denoted with a MMSI number.

[2] In the event of a communication failure, difficulties or other safety factors, the Center may direct or permit a user to monitor and report on any other designated monitoring frequency or the bridge-to-bridge navigational frequency, 156.650 MHz (Channel 13) or 156.375 MHz (Ch. 67), to the extent that doing so provides a level of safety beyond that provided by other means. The bridge-to-bridge navigational frequency, 156.650 MHz (Ch. 13), is used in certain monitoring areas where the level of reporting does not warrant a designated frequency.

[3] All geographic coordinates (latitude and longitude) are expressed in North American Datum of 1983 (NAD 83).

[4] Some monitoring areas extend beyond navigable waters. Although not required, users are strongly encouraged to maintain a listening watch on the designated monitoring frequency in these areas. Otherwise, they are required to maintain watch as stated in 47 CFR 80.148.

[5] In addition to the vessels denoted in section 161.16 of this chapter, requirements set forth in subpart B of 33 CFR part 161 also apply to any vessel transiting VMRS Buzzards Bay required to carry a bridge-to-bridge radiotelephone by part 26 of this chapter.

[6] Until otherwise directed, full VTS services will not be available in the Calcasieu Channel, Calcasieu River Channel, and the ICW from MM 260 to MM 191. Vessels may contact Port Arthur Traffic on the designated VTS frequency to request advisories, but are not required to monitor the VTS frequency in this sector.

[7] A Cooperative Vessel Traffic Service was established by the United States and Canada within adjoining waters. The appropriate Center administers the rules issued by both nations; however, enforces only its own set of rules within its jurisdiction. Note, the bridge-to-bridge navigational frequency, 156.650 MHz (Ch. 13), is not so designated in Canadian waters, therefore users are encouraged and permitted to make passing arrangements on the designated monitoring frequencies.

NOTES

NOTES

NOTES